IMPROV
YOURSELF

IMPROV YOURSELF

Business
Spontaneity
at the
Speed of Thought

Joseph A. Keefe

John Wiley & Sons, Inc.

Published by John Wiley & Sons, Inc., Hoboken, New Jersey.
Published simultaneously in Canada.

For general information on our other products and services please contact our Customer Care Department within the U.S. at (800) 762-2974, outside the United States at (317) 572-3993 or fax (317) 572-4002.

Wiley also publishes its books in a variety of electronic formats. Some content that appears in print may not be available in electronic books. For more information about Wiley products visit out web site at www.Wiley.com.

Designations used by companies to distinguish their products are often claimed by trademarks. In all instances where the author or publisher is aware of a claim, the product names appear in Initial Capital letters. Readers, however, should contact the appropriate companies for more complete information regarding trademarks and registration.

Library of Congress Cataloging-in-Publication Data:

Keefe, Joseph A.
　　Improv yourself : business spontaneity at the speed of thought /
Joseph A. Keefe.
　　　p.　cm.
　　Includes bibliographical references and index.
　　ISBN 0-471-21638-0 (cloth : alk. paper)
　　1. Creative ability in business.　2. Organizational change.　3. Problem
solving.　4. Risk management.　5. Creative thinking.　I. Title.
　HD53 .K43　2002
　650.1—dc21　　　　　　　　　　　　　　　　　　　2002011152

Printed in the United States of America.

10　9　8　7　6　5　4　3　2　1

Contents

CONTENTS

Acknowledgments

The great teachers in my life are directly responsible for this book and every piece of art or commerce I will ever create. They are the ones who inspire as well as lead us. Through passion for their subjects and students they turn dull to bright and boring to not. My great teachers were, in no special order: Richard and Mary Keefe, Dr. William J. Peterman, Bernie Sahlins, Joyce Sloane, Jo Forsberg, David Shepherd, Diana Montez, and Douglas Adams. Each one of them made the subjects fun and my life and comedy better. (I hold them all legally responsible.)

Over the years, I've been lucky enough to work with a group of associates who've become more than friends; we've developed this strangely functional family of improv, comedy, and production artists. They are, past and present: Teresa Goodwin, Kristina Chamberlain, Darren Critz, Carmen Baumgardner, Emily Dorezas, Kevin Fleming, Liz Cackowski, Richard Laible, Mark

Belden, Rick Hall, Renee Albert, Bret Scott, Tom Purcell, Rachel Hamilton, Kevin and John Farley, Tracy Thorpe, my brothers and sisters (the original comedy ensemble), and many more old friends.

Profound appreciation to Dan Santow for jumping in when jumping of all kinds was sorely needed. My special gratitude to Pat Friedlander for the years of faith and trust—and for helping me close some deals. Also wonderful thanks to Dr. Michelle Studl for all the stress management techniques and consultation on the subject matter.

I also send my immense gratefulness to all the players on all the stages that I was lucky enough to work with—especially that wonderfully wacky institution, *The Second City*.

My deepest thanks and love go to Andrew, Johnny, and especially Karen, who make every day more fun than can be imagined.

Foreword

There's this man who has grown discontented with his life. He's bored by his job, dissatisfied with his house, and tired of his wife. One day, while walking past a construction site, he is struck on the head by a falling beam and knocked out. Upon waking he can remember nothing not even his name — but he is filled with an exhilarating sense of freedom and an urgent desire to escape. Finding several hundred dollars in his pants pocket (his wallet, which held all his credit cards and other identifying information, was stolen while he lay unconscious), the man buys a plane ticket, flies across the country, and settles in a new city. Within a year he has a new job doing exactly what he used to do, he is living in a new house almost identical to his old one, and he is engaged to a woman who could be the twin of his former wife.

I can't recall who wrote this particular story, which I must have read at least 20 years ago (today, of course, the requirement to produce six kinds of identification to buy a plane ticket pushes the whole premise into the realm of science fiction). But the tale's message about human nature is timeless. We are embracers of the familiar, rejoicers in the stable, smug plodders through ruts of our own making. Plagued as we are today by threats to our security and to our securities, the desire to mitigate risk and forestall change is stronger than ever. Safety first, last, and always. Look both ways before doing anything.

Funny thing, though: While as individuals we shun risk, as a culture we celebrate it. This is particularly true in business. The dot-coms have sunk into the tar pits of history, yet entrepreneurs—those consummate risk takers—are still held in generally high esteem. Within large companies, managers—clearly oblivious to the irony of leveraging cliché against stasis—urge employees to think outside boxes and push envelopes. Bold actions are applauded, baby steps derided. Forget those little tasting spoons they pass out at Baskin Robbins, exhort the experts. Plunk down your money for a triple-dip bubble-gum-pop-rocks-and-root-beer-flavored cone and be damned!

From outside comes pressure to take risks. From inside comes the urge to climb into bed and watch reruns on TV Land, or maybe switch to a less demanding career as a hairnet professional. This, then, is the question: If we accept that risk in business is inevitable, can we train ourselves to ignore its terrors, to embrace its opportunities, and to maneuver around its hairpin curves with the speed and grace of Formula One racers? Is there a tool for something like that?

Yes, says Joe Keefe, and its name is improvisation. And no, improv isn't just a theater thing. Indeed, it is difficult to imagine a profession in which it isn't sometimes necessary to rapidly conjure a coherent, compelling whole from vague and chaotic fragments. Think of your favorite college professor, standing noteless at the podium, leading 200 clueless undergraduates in discussion with the assurance of an orchestra conductor. Think of those cooks on *Iron Chef* who invite themselves into people's homes and concoct gourmet repasts out of a can of tomato soup, a tin of sardines, and three slightly furry plums. Think of the action hero, bound hand and foot and tossed from a dirigible, who manages to catch his belt buckle on a protruding spar, sever the ropes with his cufflinks, tie the pieces together and use them to climb back on board, knock out a passing guard, steal his uniform, and ultimately impale the villain on his very own hand which happens to be a steel hook (action heroes are always given lots of stuff to improvise with).

In business, think of the great brainstormers. The great rapid prototypers. The great public speakers. The great team leaders. The great innovators. All are masters of improvisation. And, says Keefe, you can be one, too.

I had the opportunity to observe Keefe and his team in action several years ago. I had heard that Second City—the undisputed wellspring of improvisational comedy and a favorite haunt when I was an undergraduate at Northwestern University—ran workshops on improvisation for business folk. Sensing a story, I flew to Chicago and spent several days watching as people wearing casual clothes and nervous expressions were flipped out of their workaday frying pans and into Keefe's peculiar brand of fire. Participants ranged from the relatively young and uninhibited crew of a child-oriented dot-com to the far stiffer, more distrustful members of a project team from a major pharmaceutical company. The latter looked like an especially uncrackable nut. For the first hour the middle managers didn't laugh at all, and the scientists laughed only when someone made a joke about lipids.

Keefe led everyone through a series of exercises—many of which are described in this book—that made greater and greater demands on participants' concentration and mental agility. As the day progressed, people relaxed and began to enjoy themselves—something you would naturally expect. But, to my surprise, they also began to get it. You could see it in their body language as colleagues leaned into one another, made eye contact more frequently, and listened as if their lives depended on it. Responses grew quicker and, often, smarter. By the time teams reached the product-selling game, described on page 102, some of their presentations were positively inspired. I can't imagine that back in the office their next meeting was quite the agenda-driven, bullet-point-scripted, senior-manager-dominated production they were accustomed to.

I've been to a number of presentations where fun-in-the-work-place experts advocated tossing around basketballs, festooning cubicles with silly string, and "putting the elf" (I can scarcely bring myself to say it) "in self." Well, this isn't that. Improv is about teaching your mind to jump the tracks. It is about learning to communicate in a manner that is the inverse of the game of telephone: As information passes from person to person it becomes more meaningful. It is about accepting risk as a desirable condition that makes the game worth playing.

It is about time to start reading the book.

—Leigh Buchanan
Senior Editor
Inc Magazine

Introduction

I love improvisation.

I love it not only because it's spontaneous idea generation, an advanced communications process, and just plain fun. I also love improv because it pays my bills—a valuable attribute for any artistically commercial discipline. It is the method I use to generate books, write plays, develop small and hilarious television shows, compose sketch comedy, create corporate shows and videos, and for much more. Improv is an amazingly rewarding source of energy, comedy, and artistry—an accessible skill that becomes a path of creative power. It also gave me my start in the comedy business for which I am eternally grateful.

Rest assured, you don't have to go into sketch comedy or jazz music to employ improv for its countless intrinsic benefits. Due to its idea generation and spontaneity building traits, the improv applications for business and life are virtually infinite. We've created improv-business applications for salespeople, lawyers, research scientists, ad agencies, doctors, airline personnel, police forces, hotel chains, sports teams, consulting organizations, social workers, telemarketers, CEOs, CIOs, MBAs, money managers, universities, and teams of every sort, structure, and style, to name just a few.

In my bizarre and sometimes brilliant career, I've led several thousand workshops for every type of organization imaginable, and some that aren't imaginable. These workshops made the attendees more at ease with creation, more spontaneous with themselves and each other, and better able to initiate and manage team needs, and allowed the participants to *have more fun* in their work and lives. By actually enjoying themselves in the experience of improv, participants are able to access new areas of individual innovation and team productivity. This is what improv does for the world.

In this book, you'll find an introductory course for improvisation with special emphasis on exercises and games that build improv-business skills. You'll also find technical background, improv theory as it relates to commerce and art, and tips for the development of personal and team spontaneity. These lessons have been gathered over decades of work with businesses around the globe. As with any good teacher or consultant, I've learned much more from my clients than I ever could have imagined. This book is a result of the bizarre decades of fun in bringing improv and a sense of humor to where it is most desperately needed — *the business world!*

Enjoy.

IMPROV
YOURSELF

CHAPTER 1

Everyone Improvises — They Just Don't Always Know It

You can improvise as most people do — for crisis management — or you can improvise as the entertainment world does — both to entertain and to create new material. The question becomes: Are you going to improvise well in order to achieve your needs and goals or are you going to improvise badly and stumble into solutions, not all of them the best they can be? The choice is yours: Do it well or do it badly. Either way, you will have to improvise now and in the future.

It's safe to say that show-biz depends on improv not only as a critical tool for product development but also as an operating mechanism for innovation and creativity management. Here are some neat examples from the entertainment world:

- Lenny Bruce had a "five-minute improv" rule. He would improvise five minutes of new, topical material in every standup comedy show he did. The logic was pristine: After revision and editing, he'd have an entirely new act every two or three months.

- Prior to the filming of a critical swordfight scene in *Indiana Jones*, Harrison Ford became ill, sick enough that he could barely stand up in order to shoot the scene. To resolve the problem and maintain the shooting schedule, Steven Spielberg had the villain pull his sword and execute a huge flourish of expert swordplay. At the conclusion of this grand display of machismo, Indy simply pulls out his gun and shoots the villain. This necessary act of improvised solution provided one of the biggest laughs of the movie, and it kept everyone on time and budget.

- John Lennon and Paul McCartney were one of the great improvising teams in recent history. Many of their compositions were born because one of the pair accepted the other's suggestions without conditions. The medley at the end of "Abbey Road" is an incredible example of not only allowing another's initiation to exist, but also supporting each initiation by synthesizing it with other diverse ideas. Each song becomes complementary to the one preceding it with the entire composition becoming significantly greater than the sum of its parts.

- On the occasion of the birth of John Lennon's son Julian, Paul McCartney wrote the classic rock anthem "Hey Jude" to celebrate the event. As is common with many artists in the midst of creation, McCartney temporarily filled in one line of the song with a specific imagery that had little direct, logical relevance to the content. The line *the movement you need is on your shoulder* was an odd image that McCartney couldn't quite understand or explain; he simply composed the line to

2

hold the space for future revision. (Similarly, when McCartney first dreamed up the song "Yesterday" the lyric in his head was scrambled eggs.) When John Lennon first heard "Hey Jude" played, McCartney apologized for the line, explaining that he would revise it later. Lennon stopped him, assuring McCartney that he understood the imagery, that it was useful, and not to change a word of the original composition. Lennon said, "I get what you're trying to say. Leave it just as it is."

In this last case, the emotional impact of the imagery was more important than the perceived failure of the line. Lennon's unhesitating acceptance of the original lyric McCartney wrote—one that seemingly had little logic or obvious meaning—not only underscored the artistic respect that they held for one another but also supported a process by which some of the best music in history was composed. Lennon and McCartney listened to each other, supported good ideas, offered new direction, and focused on continual creation as their operating methodology. This is the process of genius. This is improvising: continuous activity based on active agreement and exploration.

Lennon and McCartney did it to entertain (and change) the world. You might do it for other reasons (though changing the world is to be encouraged). It just doesn't matter: I improvise; you improvise; we all improvise. Why not do it the best you can?

WHY LEARN TO IMPROVISE?

You're pretty smart. You mostly know what you're talking about and the times when you haven't got a clue, you're pretty good at faking it until the clue comes to you. By virtue of the fact that you've actually bought or borrowed this book, you have an obvious interest in business and enough room on your credit card to cover the charge, which means you're probably okay with money. Most of you have graduated from elementary and high school and most likely college, as well. So you've made it to a level that provides just enough intellectual and karmic discomfort to keep you on your toes.

It's safe to say that everyone improvises at some time in his or her daily life (anyone who commutes to work improvises just to get there on time). And yet, with all the training, education, and experience you've managed to gather over the years, most of you have never even thought to study improvisation as a communication or art form. This is not to say that you don't improvise very well; many of you are already brilliant improvisers, but you probably don't know specifically *how* or *why* you improvise—you just do it when you have to, spontaneously and without thinking much about it.

What do I mean when I say that you improvise in your daily life "spontaneously and without thinking much about it"? Well, every process breaks down eventually, creative applications run out of steam, only half of your stuff shows up at the pitch and you've got to make the sale with what you have. In these moments of crisis, we seek solutions through a virtually limitless supply of options, which are improvised. We:

- Revise strategy to fit available resources.
- Acquire alternate means to achieve results.
- Remanage our audience's (and our own) expectations to fit new parameters.
- Stretch old resources to fit new needs.

4

You're supposed to implement improv when needed, harnessing its forces and directing them toward useful results. And yet, you've had no formal training in the discipline of improvisation. It's ironic, but you're expected to make everything up as you go along.

Well, not anymore: Welcome, my friend, to your formal training in improv. Our job will be to provide the basics of improv, lay out a lesson plan for experiential involvement, and share theories that have direct applications in business and innovation. And we're going to *have fun* doing it. (That's a nonironic promise.)

BUILDING THE SKILLS

By applying improv techniques in practice sessions and workshops, you and your colleagues will increase your "improvabilities":

- The ability to think and act on your feet.
- The talent to respond to changing circumstances.
- The facility to change circumstances to fit needs.
- Superior idea generation and brainstorming skills.
- Speed and flexibility in crisis management.
- Spontaneity.
- Applying a sense of humor when and where needed.

Our lessons contain theory and exercises that will expose you to experiential improv. Simply put, you will understand the concepts and applications, but it will take consistent practice to embed improvability in your business and personal life. As with all learning, there is no substitute for experience, and with improv, it's better that you get the experience in workshops and creative sessions, instead of in front of the client.

As with any art form, there is effort involved in the mastery of the craft. The rewards, though, are deep and lasting. Improv frees your mind, makes teamwork stunningly easier, and helps you get better ideas. Heck, anything that makes your business life a little better and more enjoyable is well worth the investment.

IMPROV DEALS WITH WHAT'S THERE

Improvisation is *not:*

- B.S.-ing or making stuff up out of thin air.
- A way to come up with a million jokes (though good improvisers are funny).
- Disorder.
- Stalling.
- The path of least resistance.

Improvisation *is:*

- Accurately assessing the needs of a given situation.
- Taking action to address relevant issues.
- Moving forward in a positive new direction.
- Working with your intuition toward useful results.
- Operating clearly in chaotic situations.
- Taking risk.
- New.

Improv is making the most of what you have and getting the most out of what you make. Improv is flexibility in rigid circumstances, movement through stagnation, and active choices instead of passive responses. It is a discipline, craft, and art form that requires a bit of time and study in order to comprehend it and incorporate it into your real and business life.

CHAPTER 2

What (the Heck) Is Improvisation (Anyway)?

In our quest to begin at the beginning, let's define the terms of our new improv language; let's understand its vocabulary. We'll eventually get to the *why* and *how* of improvisation, but first we address the *what*.

So, what the heck *is* improv, anyway? It's simplest to describe improvisation as a course of action taken when normal procedures aren't working or as alternative systems to which we turn when regular systems aren't generating the intended results. In other words: *We're stuck in the same old/same old. We've been down this path before.*

Furthermore, we improvise not only when things aren't working but also when we feel at risk or threatened. *We're lost in the woods. It's getting dark and cold. Let's make a lean-to from these branches and then build a fire from your toupee.*

This is only one way to say it. There are many others, and I'm going to articulate them as we go along. Why am I giving you more than one way to define it? Does improvisation have that many meanings? Well, yes and no. It's so important that you understand what improv is that I'm going to say it in as many ways as possible, so if by chance you're having trouble understanding and accepting the way it's worded in one example, there's another example waiting to clarify. The goal is to understand; if you have to read a few extra paragraphs to get there, so much the better. At least by the end we'll all be on the same page — literally, figuratively, and with total understanding.

Okay, enough caveats: Here's another mouthful of a definition: Improvisation is a path/toolset through which players generate products, compositions, or activities by accessing intuitive processes for spontaneous results. Improvisation is an art form through which people manage spontaneously generated ideas, inspirations, and moments (sometimes directed to an end result). Improvisation is a toolset to create and explore intuitive processes for dynamically spontaneous experiences. Improvisation as an art form can be demonstrated as music, theater, comedy, drama, literature, and virtually every creative medium. Improvisation is a form by which everything from moments of excruciatingly beautiful art to life-saving actions may be achieved. Improvisation occurs everywhere:

- Firefighters string together apparatus to pluck a flood victim from a raging river (team improvisation).
- A politician issues a quick and witty retort to an unexpected question. (Okay, this is admittedly rare, but experts spend years teaching public figures how to be "spontaneous.")
- Basketball players improvise physical movement for specific results. Defying many laws of gravity, an athlete's

game-winning shot is improv problem-solving under intense pressure. Players with higher improvisational skills succeed because they are, by definition, harder to stop in their athletic quests.

IMPROV PLAYERS

By learning and refining improv skills, improv players enhance many abilities and traits that are useful in the business and real world.

- *Being "in the moment."* Improv forces our concentration into the immediate here and now. (This concept will be relentlessly drilled into your helpless psyches from now on.)
- *Seeing what's here.* Improvisation begins where you are; you work with what you have now; you don't wait for anything else to arrive.
- *Responsiveness.* Players don't wait for good ideas. They act now until the good ideas or "initiations" are generated. And they deal with other players' initiations as agreeably and well as with their own ideas.
- *Spontaneity.* Improv players *always* move to action. Logical considerations are not nearly as important to a real player as the emotional and actionable moments in front of them.

WE FEEL, THEREFORE WE IMPROVISE

Intuitively, most humans recognize the essential need for improvisation—after all, it's an important survival mechanism. Anyone who's ever shocked himself by swerving as if on autopilot to avoid a car accident or who has smart-allecky teenagers knows the inherent value, the vital necessity, of improvisation. Most of us not only recognize the need for improv but also understand the importance of refining our improv skills. (The fact that you're reading this book is our first clue.)

While we all would like to become better improvisers, we expect that our leaders be great improvisers, even if we don't think about it exactly in those terms. It's not an understatement to say that great leaders and doers, whether or not we like or respect them, attain greatness through their intuitive ability to access improvisation (think Churchill; think Bill Gates; think Evita the woman, not the musical). A combination of tenacity, improv skills, brains/smarts, and a skillful use of timing are the hallmarks of great leaders. If you aspire to great leadership, a basic understanding of improvisation is as important as courage. Read on, leader; we'll get you there.

THE STATE OF IMPROVISING, PART I

We start with a logical choice to tap into emotional states. Improvisers develop highly attuned decision-making processes to act on impulses, senses, intuition, directions, and so forth. Improvisers always *move* to action, consciously eliminating comparatively easy concepts like "rejection" or "acceptance," and cultivating finely developed intuitive choices for direction and exploration.

Consider this important thought: Improvisation combines the *act of composition* with the *end results*. In other words, *the activity and the object of the activity are one in the same.* Creation and productivity merge to form one product: continuous creation.

Improv demands activity. At the risk of damaging a major Zen philosophy, you gotta be doing it to be doing it. The creation is the performance; the performer is the author; the idea is the show. This is the definition of "being in the moment" or "being present." It's the embodiment of present concentration while actively incorporating new ideas and information. Improvisation is being here now. Improv is being in *this* here and in *this* now.

BRIEF DIGRESSION

Viola Spolin, author of *Improvisation for the Theater*, and a guiding light of theatrical improvisation, suggested that "to improvise is to fail." The idea is that to improvise correctly, one must be willing to risk rejection and more. Improvisers must accept a willingness to risk and fail, then risk again.

The willingness to ignore traditional concepts of success and failure, on a conscious level, is critical to proper improv development. "Failure" in the traditional sense is immaterial to the improvising process. It must be ignored during the process. For that matter, traditional "success" is just as useless. Because analysis draws out attention from the present to the past, from activity to passivity, judgments of any kind must be suspended in the current activity/present tense. The suspension of internal/external judgment allows us to improvise actively and functionally, pursuing radical choices, paths, and ultimately, results.

Improvisation is activity. The process and the end result are the same thing. The conceptual notions of success and failure exist in judgment. Judgment is reactive. It occurs after the fact. When you're improvising correctly, you can't actually *be* failing. Technically, failure can occur only after improvisation stops. So we separate the judgment process from improvising activity because not only are they necessarily mutually exclusive, but to introduce one into the other stops both.

Continuing with the definition theme: *Improvisation is current, active concentration on a task while incorporating new information for that task*. This is more important than "thinking outside the box" (we destroy the box and act outside the remnants). Improvisation is teaching yourself new behavior, a new way to work, a new way to exist. As we incorporate the new stimuli and information from the improv activity, the activity itself mutates and recomposes in unknown directions. We trust our intuitive instincts to take us somewhere useful, interesting, and challenging. We walk the tightrope of our own minds and hearts.

Quite literally, when improvising, your heart is a much better guide than your head. You *feel* improvisation on a very basic level. This leads us to a *business productivity dichotomy* —in the business world people assume that *feeling* something is bad, that emotion is inappropriate. In our improv path, we're going to embrace the opposite notion. We're going to allow ourselves to be uncomfortable and to revel in our uneasiness.

The awkward feeling of "something new" is exactly the impetus that will spur brains and hearts to novel, unusual, different, strange, innovative results. "Comfortable" is your standard operating procedure that leads to normal ideas and average activity. Improvisation leads you to the weird, different, odd, inspired, wild, nonnormal: You're now stretching outside your limits.

STRANGE IS USEFUL

Improvisation makes strange bedfellows. It not only promotes unusual association of ideas, but also demands relationships between diverse concepts. Improvisation links weird notions to even weirder ones. Again, as improvisers we are taught to *move toward this impulse.* The syllogism will change from $a + b = c$ to $@ + m =$ fish.

Improvisers find security in the continual exploration of risks. A major improv rule is "Follow the fear and it will set you free." Like a firefighter moving to a fire, improvisers face the risks of spontaneous creativity. Through the repetition of improvisational creative processes, artists burn out the fear of rejection; as fear diminishes, productivity and quality increase. Improvisers embrace the activity as opposed to the results. It's all about the moments, the work, the jazz. As Grandpa Wallenda said, "Life is on the wire; all else is waiting."

BRIEF AND WORDY DIGRESSION

It's important to clarify contextual excellence and its impact on improvisation versus improv as a skill-building toolset. Jazz improvisers master complex progressions, scales, and instrumentation as part of their increasing ability to improvise. Their technical skill increases the ability to improvise well. Having contextual excellence, and aspiring to it, is important in improvisation, but not essential.

During playtime with my two brilliant, almost-teen sons, we incorporate many improv games. I initiate a story, such as, "There once was a huge dragon who lived _____ . . ." and point to my sons to fill in the blank. The stories are entertaining, many times hilarious and excellent improvisation. The boys need no training or contextual excellence to improvise at an extremely high level. Their only requirements are to follow basic rules: Listen, agree, add, accept. Through this process of initiation, agreement, acceptance, and exploration, they experience creation, improv, and problem solving, and they're also partaking in the sheer joy of comedy fun.

Through the continuous practice of risk, improvisers learn that "success" exists *only within the process itself*. If you're doing it well, you're doing it well; if you're not, you're not. The intuitive connection an artist makes with her work, in the moment it's being generated, is much more important than the end results. Improvisers play for themselves first and share the action with the audience almost as an afterthought. First, improvisers must please themselves.

Gale Sayers, Chicago Bears legend, was improvisation in action. There are replays of Sayers eluding as many as nine opponents on his way to the end zone. Yet when asked *how* he did it, Sayers was unable to describe the conscious process of his improvised movements. He simply did it. You must become free; you must free yourself to improvise well.

INTUITION

To improvise, we move away from logic and into intuitive emotion; logical thinking directly blocks improvisation. Logic itself is analytical processing of information. In order to analyze, we must stop and shift activity from creation to review. As we've already defined, the activity and end results of improvisation are one and the same, so analyzing it stops it. We move from memory—drawing on prior actions, experiences, and activities—into current experience—immersing ourselves in the here and now.

TOSS OUT AUTHORITY

Being in the moment, being in current experience, means that you can't retain the shield of authority or expertise or comfort.

You must step away. You must risk; hazards must be present. To improvise without risk is oxymoronic—it can't be done. Improvising is an experience of continual challenge. In other words: risk-challenge, risk-challenge, risk-challenge.

- You don't like to speak in front of people = You will speak in front of people.
- You're "not creative" = You will create.
- You don't like being uncomfortable = You must become uncomfortable.

Comfort is normal. It's what you're used to. Being comfortable means you're doing what you always do. Improvising begins by being uncomfortable. When you're starting on your improv journey, here are some of the voices that begin to occupy your head:

This is weird . . .

What are they doing?

I've never done that . . .

I'm not used to this kind of stuff.

You feel uncomfortable improvising? Great. Now you're doing something new, something unusual, something worthwhile.

THE STATE OF IMPROVISING, PART II

The components of improv are:

- *A clear mind.* Improvisation begins with conceptions that occur in the immediate moment. To allow for these conceptions to develop naturally, begin with clarity—not necessarily a literal state of nothingness, but a mind cleared of extrane-

IMPROV/THEATER

In the world of theater, improvisation is employed for a wide variety of functions:

- Developing a character from the context of its biography. This is done through a wide range of exercises:
  - Assume the life of your character and interact in rehearsal or in public. This allows the actor to understand and further develop the character.
  - Share stories of the character's past experiences.
  - Immerse the character in unusual or unexpected situations and circumstances.
- Building history between two characters by interacting in situations outside the script.
- Developing a sketch, scene, script, or entire production through the use of characters' action, behavior, and interaction in various environments.

Tactically, the uses of improvisation in any creative endeavor range as far as the imagination of the creator. Once you've immersed yourself in improv processes, you begin to build new improv applications for as many areas as you have interest. Improv techniques carry over from theater to music to art and more. The art of improv is applicable across the spectrum of creativity.

ousness. (It helps to turn off your mobile phone and beeper and to leave your *PDA* at home. Don't tell your assistant where you can be reached.)

- *Intuitive occurrence.* A thing presents itself for action and development. The thing can be an idea, a movement, a thought, a response, or whatever. The occurrence arrives from the clear mind or from an external stimulus or context.

- *Action.* We move to act on the occurrence, complementing it, forwarding it. In the classic term of improvisation, we "heighten and explore" this occurrence.
- *Offering.* We offer the activity and occurrence to our partners for further exploration. We agree to agree on the activity.
- *Accepting.* We accept the dynamic action of our partners and add to it.
- *Continuing.* We explore the many facets of our action until it's run its course—then run the course just a little longer.

Fish don't consider swimming; they just swim. Birds fly; lions lie. Eliminate the anxiety of improvisation, remove your self-doubts and improvisation becomes natural. Most of us suffer through improvisation because for whatever reason we won't clear our minds to truly allow it to exist. If you allow improvisation, it will allow you.

STEPS TO GET THERE

There are steps that must be taken to improvise:

1. *Create context.* In order to develop a scene, we first generate characters to inhabit it.
2. *Immerse in environment.* The physical (or nonphysical) environment is explored and heightened, establishing a connection and groundwork for the character interaction.
3. *Hyperactively listen.* This is one of the most critical components of improvisation (and into which we'll delve in more detail later on). It may be said that improvising *cannot exist* without listening—to your improv partners, to the music you're

generating, or to any of the other myriad needs of the creation. Consider listening the way an actor must listen onstage:

- *Physical preparation.* Actors must turn to each other (unless specifically blocked otherwise).

- *Each moment is new, right now.* An actor's job is the fresh creation of an immediate experience occurring right now. Many "method" acting techniques focus on cultivating an actor's ability to "be in the moment, right now." That is, they must be discovering the activity *as it unfolds before them.* Any deviation, any slip-up in this concentration is immediately evident to the audience because the mistake violates their suspension of disbelief.

- *Actors must listen to comprehend meaning rather than listen simply to respond!* Actors continually train themselves to listen to understand the person speaking as opposed to just waiting for them to finish. (The world will be a much better place when we all embrace this trait.)

  How many times have you been in situations where you know that the person to whom you're speaking is listening only enough to figure out if you're saying something that he's already thinking? He just wants you to say what he's already decided. This all-too-prevalent scenario destroys improvisation, as well as most solid decision making, not to mention many marriages.

4. *Add to the exercise.* Improvisers, in team contexts, must add to the process as equally as possible. No one person is allowed to stand outside the creative event. (Certainly team members may be alternated in and out of exercises, but the time in creative process must be as equal as possible. Remember: In addition to the specific goals of any exercise, you are also building the skills of individual team members.)

5. *Agree.* Once the context is established, the team members must agree to it in the context and activities of the creative process. It's not fair to destroy the idea at work because you came up with a different one. Different ideas are recorded and managed in their turn.

6. *Accept.* Each person in the team context must accept the group results as *at least as valuable as their own.* Again, no standing outside the group process and thinking, "I've got a better idea than this one." It's your responsibility to raise the idea in the context of the group process. Addition and acceptance of ideas is the only way that progress can be made. Standing outside and judging the process damages it.

These components are the basis for team improvisation. The degree to which they're nurtured will increase teamwork success. Conversely, if any of the components are abused or absent, team constructions falter or fail completely.

THE STATE OF IMPROVISING, PART III

Improv is:

- *A blank slate, an uncarved block, a tabula rasa.* The state of improvising is an open channel, allowing intuition to move in and out of context without obstruction.
- *Intuitive.* Accurate, state-of-mind improvisation allows for activity as it develops and is needed.
- *Immediate.* Improvisation itself does not demand results. The context in which improvisation is set may have the expectation of results, but improv itself doesn't need results to exist. Improvisation needs only itself, motivation, and risk.

The results generated from improvisation (the end product) and the means of improv (the activity) are one and the same. When improvising correctly, the *end result is the activity itself.* Conversely, if an end result is forced onto the improvisation, it skews the results and process into other forms. If you're going to operate in an intuitive state, you can't force direction on the state.

Improvisers become a conduit for the energy that they, themselves, are in the process of creating and expending. When you're improvising well, you get the feeling that there's more energy than normal in action, and that you're consciously controlling only part of it. If improvisation can be experienced only in this immediate time and space, it follows that improvisers must also be present and current in this time and space. This demand is constant and immediate in improvising. You simply must be in this moment to create. If your concentration lies elsewhere, you can't improvise here and now.

Having said that, distractions are not the end of improvising if one can include the intrusion into the moment. Improvisers incorporate stimuli as they go. So go and incorporate.

CHAPTER 3

Things You Need to Know to Start Improv-ing

SOME BASICS AND SOME PHILOSOPHY

We're going to jump right in, so if you haven't been paying attention up to this point, you'll be left behind (just kidding).

Since the demands, criteria, and mechanisms of what it means to be a "business success" evolve daily, sometimes moment-to-moment, you have no assurance that what worked yesterday will work this morning, let alone tomorrow. It may, but it may not; even so, you just can't count on it. The only real security is in the certainties that schedules will get shorter, budgets will get tighter, and your understanding of emerging technology is reduced in exact proportion to its critical value.

So organizations must evolve to succeed, evolution is change, you must change, and you must assist those around you with change or they will not buy you bagels when it's their turn.

21

Transformation is the currency of future business. Success will come to those who not only can and are willing to adapt, but lead in adaptation.

Evolution is necessary and inevitable. On the one hand, transformation is difficult by its very nature—it occurs uncomfortably, for better or for worse. On the other hand, while it's important to adapt and assimilate in order to stay (at least) current with the world around us, it's not necessarily useful to change simply for its own sake. You'd like to know, or at least guess, where it is that you're going—that's called transformation with vision, value, and direction.

However, change for its own sake is still better than no change at all. This is a sacrosanct "Joe's Rule" in the world of improvisation—as soon as you get too comfortable with your situation, toss everything up in the air. If you don't, sooner or later everything will be tossed for you (or worse, *at* you).

We cling to our need for security: Different is good when different leads us to usefulness; different is bad when we've changed what worked very well in the first place. The ability to judge the differences between (and implement the results of) these two positions is the stuff of business success.

Through the careful study and application of excellent improv techniques, we learn to intuitively distinguish between useful and useless change. We learn to make constructive choices by purposefully employing intuition, creative activity, and risk-taking. These are the goals and attributes of improvisation.

WHAT JOE DOES

I'm going to share a bit about me so you know from whence I come, what I do, and why you should listen.

22

My mission is to bring improv and a sense of humor to the business world. Improvisation is an agent and process of change. I help people change. Typically, this change involves opening up brains and hearts to access new ideas and directions. I start by imparting the improv religion to team members and then we work on company-wide applications. By embracing improv as an operating modality, I promise that organizations become more nimble, responsive, and creative. That's what I do for people.

Companies come to me to implement small change. I am a small-change guy. (This is no insult in my world—all great changes start small.) Organizations ask me to provide the catalyst, tools, and permission to restructure pathways among their associates or between the company and the marketplace—from old processes and ideas to new ones. I help people and messages get across to other people through new messaging. I do this by employing several devices:

- *Improvisation:* the ability to create something where there was once nothing.
- *Chaos:* shaking the snow globe for everyone and letting the flakes fall in new ways and new places. (I like the snow globe analogy and will use it several times throughout this book. Think about it. When you shake a snow globe those flakes never fall the same way, or in the same place, twice.)
- *Humor:* opening up brains and attitudes through a functional sense of play and a playful sense of function.

These are the tools of my trade, the path-finding instruments and vehicles I wield to point and move groups in new, uncharted directions and destinations. When done well (and it always is), my job is a combination of ship's captain, Caribbean cruise direc-

23

tor, smart-aleck MBA-type biz-guy (with a heart), deep-space explorer, and Borscht Belt comic. Under my direction:

We move quickly because fast movement is better than slow.

We move often because it shakes people up.

We always move because we find ideas in energy.

We move all the time because we see different things that way.

My job, when all is said and done, is to move *you*.

I am a proven guru. I attended Guru School and graduated second in my class. (The guy ahead of me now owns Guatemala.) More importantly, I know my stuff. I literally grew up in business. My father is a very successful real estate developer, and my mother (with my dad's help) raised eight kids (talk about your fast-paced, constantly changing medium-sized business). I produced my first theatrical show when I was 12 and I've been doing it ever since. I've produced more than 3,500 shows in my career (no kidding). The great majority of the shows I produce are one-hitters, designed for specific single events such as a show for 6,000 Kraft Foods associates for a mammoth sales rally, a customized training video for John Deere Company, or a comedy extravaganza for Cadillac auto dealers. Obviously, this level of production demands a lot of casts, writers, directors, tech personnel, and more. My company is a team-building organization by design, by necessity, and by the very nature of theater itself.

THE ACT OF IMPROVISATION: COMEDY

In addition to my family environment, I grew up in the comedy business—at Chicago's world-famous Second City Theater. The founder, Bernie Sahlins, gave me my first break in show-biz and he's still regretting it (so he tells anyone who will listen).

Second City is the finest place in the world to learn the craft of comedy and the art of improvisation. When you're in a cast there, in addition to the regular, prescripted sketch show you do every night, you also improvise brand-new comedy six nights a week, every week. It's a very powerful experience because you not only have to be good, you have to be good every night for a long time. It teaches you to become continuously creative.

THE WORK OF IMPROV: A FANTASY EXAMPLE

Picture it: You're standing on a stage facing an audience of 350 strangers. You have one partner, a fellow player, with whom you share an otherwise empty stage. Hot stage lights paint your forehead a very warm yellowish white, which serves only to highlight the sweat that beads up on it. Expectations run high in the audience. After all, each person squished in at a tiny round café table in the audience has already fulfilled his or her two-drink minimum and they've just seen an incredibly fast-paced prescripted sketch show that has amazed and astounded them with its clever, rapid-fire range of sketch comedy. They've seen the funny scripted sketch material and now, as is the norm after the guaranteed-funny scripted portion of the show, they want to see true-blue improv, what I like to call comedy's version of the high-wire act *without a net*.

The buzz of improv: The audience never knows what will happen. It *can't* know what will happen because the players themselves don't know. The audience has seen the eight-by-ten black-and-white glossy pictures of former cast members in the theater lobby: Alan Alda, Bill Murray, John Belushi, Mike Myers, and way too many others to name. The audience expectations are high and justifiably so—this is where a lot of comedy careers began. They expect *you* to be the next big star so they can boast to colleagues and friends later on that they knew you when, that they saw you when you were nobody, before you were somebody, before you were you. It's part of the comedy fun.

Even though you've worked for most of your professional theatrical career (minimum 10 years) to get to this exact spot, you lock external concerns out of your mind. Random thoughts, even your ego, don't matter. Most jitters are long gone, anyhow. It's the adrenaline you live on.

Yes, the audience matters. After all, it's more satisfying to improv *for* someone than to do it on your own. But you're not here just for the audience. You're here for the other players, for the funny, and you're *always here* for the improvisation, the art of creating something out of nothing, to generate comedy where there once was none. This is a noble mission—the world needs comedy—but more important to the moment, your job is to razor-sharpen the work, the scene, the character, and the improv itself. Hone in, dig down, focus totally on the moment. You are aware of the audience—it's there but it's not really there. The improv moment demands your time and attention. Anything less is not the work; lack of concentration kills the scene and strangles it.

Okay, enough already. Right now, it's time to improvise.

Action! Your partner asks the audience for a location in which you will base your improv sketch. A couple of dozen ideas are shouted out, but the first one audibly identified was "goat farm!"

It's an important rule of improv to accept *the first suggestion offered*. The rule is to accept every suggestion without judgment, to embrace the offering as it exists—so you accept it without reservation. Employing a selection process on the list of offerings is judgmental by its very nature. To truly accept, without reservations, you must act with what's offered. As well, the first suggestions from the audience are usually of a purer nature. Ask and you shall receive. Ask well and you shall receive well.

Next, you request an opening line of dialogue and another couple-dozen screams ring out. The first distinct line is "Jerry, where's the cat?" Nothing exists yet except these two disparate suggestions. The audience suggestions place you and your partner in situations that are odd, bizarre, and unrelated—all the better for the comedy. By asking for and accepting audience suggestions, your viewers have become privileged participants in this creative improv process. They *want* to place you in a tough situation to see how you manage to navigate your way through it. This is the job of the audience and it relishes the integral involvement. All those people out there in the dark enjoy cornering you into seeming comical impossibilities.

To begin the improv process, you shed any concerns over the degree of comical difficulty inherent in the suggestions—you don't bother yourself about ease or difficulty because it's immaterial to the work. *You focus on the doing, not the worrying.*

The gently adversarial positioning (Audience vs. Players) is helpful to the comedy. The higher the audience sets the bar, the larger the success when quality comedy work is achieved.

You begin the improvised sketch:

YOU: Jerry, where's the cat?
PARTNER: Promise you won't be mad at me.

You connect to a direction offered by your partner. The scene had begun with something good and fun. The subtext, the meaning underneath the words, strongly indicates that your partner's done something wrong, perhaps even comically inappropriate. Through the request, the audience has created a character with slightly lower personal status than you (good going, audience!). The scene has begun well.

> YOU: I won't be mad at you unless you've eaten the cat.
> PARTNER: (*Much relieved*) Okay then. I didn't eat the cat.
> YOU: So?
> PARTNER: So what?
> YOU: So where's the cat?
> PARTNER: Promise you won't be mad at me?
> YOU: I've already told you I won't be mad at you.
> PARTNER: I ate the cat.
> YOU: (*Angry*) "What? That's insane. You're a goat! Goats don't eat cats."
> PARTNER: You promised you wouldn't be mad at me.
> YOU: Unless you ate the cat and you've clearly done exactly that.
> PARTNER: You just rhymed. Very nice!
> YOU: "Don't try to wriggle out of this. For a goat, you're a pig.

There are 350 people watching you work, sharpen, and hone in on the moment. This is a serious test of improvability—working without a comedy net in front of a large crowd. This is also where the true craft of comedy lives: in action, in sensing the intuitive and subconscious, in reading your partner's intention, in sensing direction, in building agreement, in working together toward an unseen yet common goal, in finding momentum, in establishing trust and emotional connection, in caring about the work, in using what's given, in heightening what's used, in challenging each other, and in loving the work as much as or more than the results. This is art as a living form.

EVERYTHING STARTS FROM NOTHING

Yes, this sketch is fictional, an improvised moment of creation put to script. In a sense, *all* fiction is improvised in the beginning; everything that exists didn't exist once. All creation is making something from nothing, doing what has not yet been done, making real what is not yet real.

When the sketch is over, the improv moment is finished: It is *so* over it's scary. Improv is like no other form of art—when you're done with it, when you've absolutely ruled the moment in a fit of visceral perfection, the whole thing is gone in a gust of experience. At the very moment you've done something wonderful, it has already puffed its way into some historical comedy memory. You might not even remember the moment as well as the audience might—its members might never forget it and it's hard for you to remember it. If you've improvised well, that's the way it works.

So you go again. This is powerful stuff—the incredible act of generating something funny out of nothing. You improvise because it's what you do. You become the form and the form becomes you.

IMPROV CREATES ITSELF

There are no masterpieces to copy, no videos to study (okay, there's *some* video but it can't tell you *how* to do it; it can only tell you what has already been done) so you study from the teachers

29

who pass down the lessons first taught by the legends of theatrical improvisation: Viola Spolin and Keith Johnstone, Del Close or Bernie Sahlins, Paul Sills or Jo Forsberg.

The lessons are passed down as by teachers in the Renaissance—they speak and move; you listen, act, and absorb. Writing on a tablet won't embed the lesson in your soul—the only useful experience is the experience itself.

You learn by doing. There is no cheating in this art form—if you're not doing it, you're not doing it. Players open themselves to risk: *Vulnerable* is the state of the improviser. You must open yourself to the risk or you end up closing your mind to the experience.

DO THIS FIRST.
DO THIS RIGHT NOW.

Chair; fire; tall; combine these three words in a sentence. (For example: The chair next to the tall lamp caught on fire.) Go ahead—blend the words into a sentence. Now, do the same activity again but create a sentence different from the first one. (For example: The tall chair fell into the fire.)

Now do it just one more time to embed the exercise: same words, new sentence. Make it as ungainly as it needs to be. (For example: Chairs that are too tall easily catch on fire.) Go ahead—one more sentence.

You have now improvised on purpose, toward a specific end result. You've created something from nothing. Or to be exact, you've created something from very little. You are now an improviser/improv-er/improvator. Welcome to a wonderful and very weird new world.

Immersing yourself in an unknown experience through unusual activity—this is improvising. Improvising is doing, acting, moving, generating.

Improv is *activity*. Not only that, but improvisation is *immediate* activity. Improvisation is always in the present moment. So I'm going to ask you to try the actions, exercises, and challenges in this book *as you first read them!* It's important that you try things out without preconceptions—to risk some activity without considering the actions before you take them. Improv is doing, so *do*.

MORE ABOUT JOE

I run dozens of seminars and workshops every year for clients around the globe. My first action in every workshop is to get people up and moving—improvising on their feet within the first three minutes that they see me. Seventy-five percent of any improv workshop is action, activity, movement, initiation, and acceptance (another 10% is eating bagels and drinking coffee). To learn, players must play. There's no substitute. We take action and learn by the actions we take.

Buckminster Fuller, the renowned philosopher, educator, and architect, lectured a lot in his later years. It was his practice, at the beginning of every lecture, to direct the attendees to pick up slats of wood, sheets of plastic, and various tools that he'd had placed in the auditorium.

"Let's build a dome," he would begin. The attendees, having expected a normal lecture where they would be sitting in rapt attention listening to a lone man perched at a lectern on a stage, would move to the materials and begin assembling them under Mr. Fuller's direction.

Frequently, he would hear small objections: "Mr. Fuller, I'm here for the lecture on architecture."

31

Fuller would reply, "How about if I talk while we build the dome? That way you can hear what I have to say while you're actually learning how to do something useful." He would communicate his theories and philosophies *while his students were actually applying them!* Buckminster Fuller was one smart guy—every class in the world should be run so well.

CHAPTER 4

Initiation/Addition/ Agreement/Acceptance/ Exploration

How's this for a sweeping statement: All improvisation, all innovation, every facet of true creativity, is based on five basic concepts:

1. Initiation.
2. Addition.
3. Agreement.
4. Acceptance.
5. Exploration.

These steps, the basics of improvisation, are also the basis for functional creative processes. If you execute these steps well, you'll inevitably become more innovative and creative. If you implement them poorly (or worse, omit a step or two), your creative processes will be flawed at best, destructive at worst.

Understanding these elements is essential to the successful

evolution of improvisation. They're the building blocks of the accurate, dynamic exchange of intuitive actions—ideas. These fundamentals are also operating principles through which groups may exchange the greatest amount of information in the shortest time possible with the least direction necessary.

When dealing with ensembles in creative processes, it's critical that every player in the group understands and accepts these steps. Ignorance or neglect of the elements leads to sporadic creative results and can alienate group members from both the process itself and other players.

When groups bicker, stagnate, or stall in creative processes, the causes can be traced back to a misunderstanding or misapplication of the basic improv components: All improvisational creativity is based on IAAAE (that's an unpronounceable acronym for Initiation, Addition, Agreement, Acceptance, and Exploration). If you're doing these, then you're improvising; if you're not, then you're not.

For groups composed for long-term creative processes or activities—innovation teams, design groups, project teams, and the like—it's important to have work discussions on the IAAAE elements, posting them for open conversation, and then establishing operating workshop guidelines to ensure players master each element.

Okay; we've hit the thesis pretty well. Now, what the heck do the actual words mean?

1. *Initiation.* Initiation is known by several aliases: action, activity, movement, startup, motivation, accident, assertion, stumble, step, and even Louise (don't ask). Call it what you will, but all creative results begin with the initiation—someone doing something (offering, writing, drawing, suggesting, moving, try-

ing, risking, etcetera-ing). In improv applications, initiations should be *physical movement* in addition to *verbal or vocal activity*. Instead of talking about it, have everyone get up, move, act out, work out about it. (This contrasts with the misguided notion that quiet, considered thought without activity or movement offers the best opportunity for ideas. Zen-like contemplation has its uses, like in the search for Nirvana, but for ensemble creation it's a practice contrary to stimulating interaction.)

JOE'S RULE

Get up and move! Do it if for no other reason than in business you just don't normally redeploy too much. By literally moving to act on ideas, you get *different* ideas. Let's not just "think outside the box." Let's move outside the box, as well.

---

2. *Addition.* Every player involved in any creative process — in fact, every person in the room during the process — must contribute to it in their turn. Build the expectation of full participation. Most importantly, all players must share their ideas and initiations with the group. Shyness, insecurity, and timidity are not valid reasons to avoid contributions to the group effort. As the game is played, everyone must play the game.

3. *Agreement.* Everyone involved in a creative process must agree on the *context* of the process, the operating rules of the work (e.g., *We will now, as a group, create a one-word story, each person contributing one word at a time to the story*). In improv, the rules of the process (though flexible) determine much of the outcome and results of the process itself. If there is uncertainty as to the play or procedure, the game becomes more difficult to play, more confused and faulty. More important, improvisation (like life) is by

35

definition chaotic enough. The function of improv will lead us to unexpected destinations, but we want to try to arrive together, as a team, as an ensemble, and preferably in one piece.

Players don't (and shouldn't and can't) agree on the *content* of the activity until it is living and evolving, but there *must* at least be agreement in the *context* of the activity. Four people rowing a boat in four different directions makes for little, if any, movement.

4. *Acceptance.* Every player involved in the process must accept every initiation, every movement, idea, and occurrence, with active, nonjudgmental acceptance. As a fellow player initiates, talks, moves, or offers an idea, it's your job to move with him, toward it, to accept the offering. Judgment or excessive consideration stops activity and places barriers to continued action. By pausing to judge or stopping activity to consider, players move from active present and future experiences into passive memory and events past. As you play, keep your concentration in the present, trust instinctive reactions to the initiation, and move with reckless abandon in the direction of the player and the activity. The river doesn't worry about where it's flowing, it just flows. Acceptance allows players to move with the current.

5. *Exploration.* Initiations stretch to fit available time and space. The slightest movement, the smallest suggestion, can lead to brilliant idea-changing directions. Typically though, we give up on great ideas *long before they give up on us.* A small, goofy idea can lead us to larger, less goofy ideas that then lead us on toward something inspired. This inspiration can lead us to greatness and venture capital interest with a sizable IPO. Almost any idea of genius started with someone who just wouldn't give up on it. Tenacious exploration is the key to greatness. Tenacious exploration of small initiations is the hallmark of excellent improvising.

36

Do not wait for the big idea, the great moment, or the ideal inspiration. Take the moment you have and make it better. Greatness will come.

IMPROVISATION IS CONTINUOUSLY APPLIED ACTION

There's another fantastically misguided perception that good ideas come from random moments of inspiration—the lightning bolt that hits us out of the blue. This is the commonly held notion that somehow if we sit still and think hard enough a great idea will appear in our brains.

This is wrong; ideas are not lightning bolts in search of your brilliance. Great ideas are *never* accidental. Great ideas happen to people who try and try to get them. Improvisation is a physical system through which players embody ideas and activities. There's very little sitting still. In fact, the few times we do sit still are intended to stimulate the need to move once again.

There's a voice of suspicion, or worse yet, resignation, in our heads that tells us that those who conjure great ideas are lucky, that smart people are just in the right place at the right time. There are other voices in our heads, too, that say, "I'm not creative. I'm not as fast or crafty as that other guy."

If we're lazy or ignorant enough, we can wait for that one brilliant lightning-bolt idea to strike us on the head, the light bulb to turn on, the *ah-ha!* moment. Waiting for an idea assures one thing: You'll be waiting for some time. Inspiration is developed through quantity and frequency of work, activity, movement, and persistent directed application of effort. In our case, we're going to improvise frequently and consistently to get more ideas faster and then turn these initiations into useful activity, which will in turn make us more money.

In order to increase our creative quality, we first must increase our creative productivity, increase the gross volume of our ideas—dozens, hundreds, and thousands more ideas than we're used to getting.

We begin by taking every necessary step to ensure that we generate and cultivate more ideas:

- Separate judgment from the creative process.
- Eliminate negative environments and external assessments.
- Develop internal and external risk-taking.
- Establish ensembles of trained, talented, and committed risk-takers.
- Build an environment of constant output.
- Support/require equal, positive contributions.
- Demand perseverance.
- Reward perseverance.
- Maintain a continuous supply of bagels, coffee, and juice.

BRIEF DIGRESSION

For most of us, perseverance is by far the most important component of radical idea generation. Perseverance equals genius. Inherently, most of us are not geniuses, so the one way we can compete is by creating dozens of ideas—through this process, we'll find the one or two ideas that have genius qualities. And then, through the generation of more and better ideas, we teach ourselves to become geniuses. No kidding—this works. I've seen undisciplined writers build themselves into brilliant comic artists. Heck, I've taught enough of them.

38

Increasing creative productivity has one incontrovertible effect on quality: *More ideas mean better ideas!* This is an immutable law of idea-generation: The more initiations you have to select from, the better the end-results of the creative process. Even when we understand this law, we create environments that inhibit it. Check the list above to see how much you support risk-taking. Do you require everyone to participate in the process? Do you support risk-taking? Do you truly reward perseverance?

MORE ON ACCEPTANCE AND AGREEMENT

The consistent and continual refinement of acceptance and agreement principles promote more and higher-quality initiations and ideas in groupwork. Agreement and acceptance practices lead to innovation and dynamic interactions. They help bond us with our fellow players. These basics also have the distinct benefit of *allowing you to accept your own ideas more readily.* The simple repetition of accepting the ideas of others allows us to accept our own ideas more easily, usefully, and functionally.

JOE'S LAW

The vast majority of creative processes that fail do so because of a judgment system applied incorrectly or too soon.

We kill our own ideas, stifling our own initiations before they've been allowed to exist. Our internal narrator says: *That idea won't work because* . . . or *I don't have good ideas* . . . or some similar cop-out. Remember, my mission is to provide you with an operating mechanism to manage change and free your powers of creative production. If we have to dig into our own heads to do it, so be it.

CHAPTER 5

Spontaneity and Responsiveness

It's likely that you bought this book to learn to become more spontaneous. Don't worry, you're far from alone—the entire world needs more spontaneity. In fact, it was very spontaneous of you to actually purchase or borrow this book. Congratulate yourself, but don't overdo it.

Improvisation is rightly renowned as an approach that frees choices of action and direction, removes obstacles to creativity, and accelerates reaction time to new stimuli (simply put, improv is spontaneity in action). Improv becomes valuable because in the normal course of our lives, and especially in the normal course of our business lives, "blocking" is a standard mode of communication.

In the business world, blocking is an all-too-acceptable condition of communication. The logic goes something like this:

BLOCKING

Blocking—inability to move, reasons why movement is prohibited.

—Webster's Dictionary

"Making the wrong choice is worse than making no choice at all."

"Let's not move; it might hurt."

"Allow us inertia; it's easier."

"Protect us from risk; it may come back to haunt us."

"Oh, please allow me sand in which to stick my head."

"Allow us to be creatively original to the extent that we look like the other guys only a little better."

These are the prayers of the Blocked and the Blockers (and sometimes the Blockheads).

One area in which the blocking tendency is especially prevalent is business communications. If you need any proof of this just think about the last corporate annual meeting you attended and you'll fully (and painfully) understand that spontaneity is drilled right out of business environments:

"Let us have no unpredictable moments, and if by chance we do have an unpredictable moment, let it be by accident!"

"In the office, ritual is prized above all else! Except in the case of bagels, the variety of which demonstrates our vast and exciting diversity of choices!"

"We want you to think out of the box, but only enough so that the things you think of closely resemble the things that we used to have *in* the box, except that they should be different from the old things in the box."

So, now we've arrived at a classic dilemma/paradox of innovation in business: In order to succeed and stay ahead of, if not at least current with, the competition, we must innovate. If we're smart and timely enough to actually lead our field, the followers must turn to new ideas in order to compete with us. Their new ideas may erode our position—our old ideas may not be staying current with changing tastes, circumstances, or economies. We must change.

But: Our old ideas were good enough to get us here in the first place. How many of them do we throw out? What do we keep? Do we melt down the whole structure and reinvent from the ground up? And what of the loyalty to the people/ideas that got us here? Do we continue to support them?

And: Can old dogs be taught new tricks? The darned process worked to get us here—what the heck are we doing when we screw around with it? How do we invigorate our colleagues and not alienate them at the same time?

And mostly . . . What about me? I'm supposed to be spontaneous now? and innovative? and new and edgy and all that crap? I'm not new and edgy—I'm old and round. Besides, I have to catch a train in half an hour.

Spontaneous activity/creative interaction defies order and normal expectations. When crafted well, spontaneity forces new perspectives and fresh approaches to old situations. When spontaneity occurs, environments change. And when spontaneity becomes a component of an environment, change becomes an accepted premise, an operating methodology.

This is often demonstrated in military training: an objective outlined, plans developed, actions initiated. Then the planners introduce variables that didn't exist in any of the preparatory stages. Same objective, but the ground has shifted; the rules have changed. The lesson for soldiers is to plan comprehensively, yet be prepared to toss plans and operate spontaneously and respond immediately to changing circumstances—*to think on their feet*.

The benefits of useful spontaneous action in military terms are obvious—you get to live instead of die. The rewards in business may not be quite so dramatic, but then again, it's all relative.

It's Personal

This note is from the Office of Redundancy Office: All spontaneity begins with *you*! Wishing that someone else would be spontaneous is like hoping someone else will live your life for you: possible, but not likely.

We all have that voice in the back of our heads whispering, "Boy, this has become predictable. I wish somebody would shake up the routine around here. Hey, hey, hey, I've got an echo in my head, head, head. . . ."

Now that I've shared your own head-voice with you, doesn't it sound goofy? You want *someone else* to be spontaneous? Fat chance, pal. So, why not *you*?

Here's an idea list:

- Institute Hawaiian Shirt Day.
- Have your co-workers bring in their last English Lit thesis from college—offer several of the fun ones for "dramatic" readings.
- Hold a meeting in the park.

- Swim.
- Display baby pictures.
- Offer unusual cheeses.
- Have Power Bars for the staff meeting.
- Conduct office chair races.

Incorporate small changes into your operating modality and the big changes not only become less gruesome, but less stop-in-your-tracks unusual.

BE THE INSTIGATOR

You be the one who changes a small thing. *You* be the one who offers the new idea. *You* be the one who cracks small and wise at the next meeting—just once, and just for effect.

Here's another idea list:

- For your next presentation, have everyone change chairs before you begin.
- In an idea session, toss a foam ball around. Whoever catches it must offer an idea: good, bad—it doesn't matter.
- At the next staff meeting, start at the agenda's end and work your way forward.

YOU HAVE MY PERMISSION

It is normal and acceptable to make spontaneity arbitrary—to instigate an unusual activity in this here and now, without prior consensus. (As you might guess, spontaneous moments work a lot better if they aren't announced in advance.) Yet impulsive moments contain some risk—they may fall flat. This is the reason why we so often avoid impulsiveness—somebody might not like it. So we stay safe: No risk = no danger.

45

We allow ourselves to find comfort in our safety. We become duller and less inventive; we work instead of play. Well, forget that stuff—force yourself to arbitrarily take a risk. You have my permission.

If you're still worried about what "they" might say, or if your attempt falls flat, I further give you permission to lay the blame on me. I doubt you're going to need to blame me, but should that come to pass, here's what you do: Get this book off your shelf, open it to this page, and allow your audience to read this passage:

JOE'S PERMISSION PASSAGE

Hi. It's me, Joe Keefe, author of this book. I gave your associate permission to be spontaneous. I accept full blame if the moment didn't work. Still, encourage your colleague to keep up the impulsive moments. In the long run, you'll all benefit from the fun. Thanks for listening. Okay, show's over. Go back to work now.

SPONTANEOUS LEADERSHIP

Leaders have a responsibility to instigate spontaneity. Organizations that desire to achieve out-of-the-boxity must embrace impulsive action from the top down. Leaders, by definition, set the implicit and explicit rules for the operations of the org. If you support and cultivate it, spontaneity will flourish. To the converse, if you react poorly, suspiciously, or controllingly, you receive those responses in return.

For leaders of an improv group, both on the stage and in the games, challenges, and exercises in this book, there is one Supreme Truth: Your initiations and your acceptance of the actions around you define the culture of your group! Let me repeat that, exclamation point and all: Your initiations and your acceptance of the actions around you define the culture of your group! Your personal suspicions, insecurities, and incapabilities directly affect your people. They will behave with the behavior they think most advantageous or acceptable. (Or they will rebel against those behaviors. Keep the rebels; they're your future.)

To draw the military analogy once more, when confronted with disaster, a leader must initiate, manage, accept, and embrace spontaneous input. When the going gets tough, the tough move quickly and nimbly. They take action. Toss out the rules and make up new ones as you go.

POSITIVITY

Spontaneous activity must contain good nature and a sense of humor. It must be motivated by a positive purpose, a useful desire. After all, impulsive actions are intended to cause delight in the recipients and instigators alike.

That deserves to be repeated: Spontaneity is intended to cause delight. It's a conscious decision to produce small moments of unexpected joy, odd pleasure, unusual amusement. A downbeat or disapproving environment quashes spontaneity—fear, insecurity, and paranoia prohibit useful impulsiveness. It's hard to be free when you feel trapped.

SPONTANEITY: THE FAQS

As we proceed in our quest for brilliant improvising and its subsequent added value to our personal and professional productivity, simple questions arise:

- Is it possible to be *too* spontaneous?
- Can someone think *too* quickly on her feet?
- Can a person be *too* witty, fast, and funny?
- Is spontaneity a sign of intelligence?
- Anchovies or not?

Joe's answers to these questions are surprisingly simple:

- No.
- No.
- No.
- Yes.
- No, thank you.

For improv purposes, it is not possible to be too spontaneous. While the results of our spontaneity may sometimes fail—some of us are human; we're going to make choices that don't work—the speed by which we achieve useful decisions, the rapidity with which we make functional choices, can't be too quick. The more we initiate spontaneity, the more we increase our ability to correctly manage it.

Improv as Spontaneous Activity

In the activity of performance improv, we act on the *first initiation first*. (This may seem a bit didactic, but trust me, it isn't.) It's essential that as an initiation occurs, we employ it immediately, actively, and constructively. Too many initial ideas are crushed simply because they were the first ones offered. We toss out the first ideas in our flawed search for the best ideas. In improvisation, we cannot allow this tendency.

Improv rules tell us that fully exploring the first offering invariably leads us to more and more ideas. We stretch, play, examine, turn over, chew on the first idea in active forms of exploration — we beat the thing like a bass drum in a marching band. We act on the first initiation first because all assertions have equal value; we don't wait for a good idea, we make the idea good.

As important, dealing with the *first* initiation quickly builds our skills at dealing with *every* initiation. We move forward through activity that builds our ability and desire to move any-where. The juice isn't in the achievement but in the activity itself; the buzz comes from brainstorming, not from the results. So we suspend our logic, move into intuition, and jump at the offering.

Here's the assertion: By increasing the speed of our initiations, we not only shorten the time necessary to achieve activity, *we also achieve better results more quickly.* When we move more quickly, when we become more spontaneous and intuitive, we get better initiations more quickly. The more nimble we become with our spontaneous initiations, the greater the volume of our initial ideas and offerings. We become good at being fast and we become fast at being good.

We increase the volume of our spontaneous actions because the increased output generates a wider range of directional choices. By increasing out ability to initiate and respond sponta-neously, we become more agile in our actions and reactions. We become more intuitive; we find security in acting more quickly; our choices become better and more useful. This is what impro-visers do for a living.

THE CONTINUING "WHY" OF SPONTANEITY

At the risk of immersing ourselves too deeply in the Zen of im-prov, the "why" of spontaneity becomes more important than the "how" or "what."

49

Spontaneous activity has intrinsic value that extends far beyond the immediate adrenaline of the moment—a sense of the unexpected, cultivation of pioneering, the grasp of challenges, and so on. To extend the logic beyond this compelling theory, *a culture that embraces spontaneity becomes, by definition, more dexterous, creative, flexible, empathetic, responsive, and functional.* It's safe to say that by including improvisation and spontaneity as an integral component of a business's operating mode, you not only make the organization better, you make it more adaptable to change and more capable of initiating change.

It's a given that efficiency in the business world usually equates to profitability. *If we know what we're doing and do what we know, we will succeed.* In the vast majority of biz-opinion, spontaneity is seen as contrary to efficiency: "We're spontaneous only when we don't know what we're doing. We change because we have to, not because we want to." We must battle this tendency to do only what we know. We must risk doing what we don't know. Hence, we begin to improvise (well, to be honest, we don't begin until Chapter 6).

CULTIVATING THE ART OF SURPRISE

Freud said a lot of really dumb things about comedy. I won't go on a rant here but, as we'll see in other Joe theories, humor serves a much greater purpose than simply rationalizing our sexuality.

As a coping mechanism alone, humor serves a noble and important function in the culture of mankind, to say nothing of the thousands of standup comics who would be forced to join therapy groups without comedy clubs in which to vent. (Hey, maybe that's why Freud analyzed jokes and their relation to the subconscious—he wanted to build a client base from all the comedians.)

However, one area where Freud came close to the mark was when it comes to the reflex of surprise in comedy and humor. Much of comedy is based on the process of leading an audience in one direction and then sharply altering the perspective or expected result. Surprising an audience builds a delight in their reactions—people love to be truly surprised. Audiences find an intense, emotional gratification in organic moments of astonishment. Laughter is one major manifestation of this surprising joy and joyful surprise.

True surprise is in sharp contrast to typically lame "surprise parties," which many people despise for the simple fact that they're rarely unanticipated or unexpected. To draw another correlation with the art of theater, when you promise an audience mystery, suspense, comedy, and/or surprise, your mission must be to truly mystify or surprise them in ways they had not contemplated or even considered. If they can see the joke coming or that the butler actually did it, the audience will not only despise you, they will tell their friends not to invest in your property. They will stay away in droves.

We have the same responsibilities to our fellow players, our teams and groups, our companies, and maybe most of all, to our *clients!* Wouldn't it be terrific if we surprised our clients with something wonderful once in a while instead of the normal unsurprising surprises: overdue shipments, misdirected creative, rising budgets, what have you?

SPONTANEOUS CONCLUSION

In order to become spontaneous, you must take action. You have my permission to fail once in a while—but like presents, with useful impulsiveness the thought is definitely as important as the

51

end result. Become motivated to be spontaneous. Make it your personal responsibility to shake up your life and the lives of those around you near and far. You'll be better for it and so will they.

UTILIZING INTUITION FOR FUN AND PROFIT

In business and life (yes, sometimes they *are* mutually exclusive), we suppress our intuition as a matter of practice. In order to convince ourselves of the validity of our ideas, we demand proof, scientific analysis, market research, focus groups, and Mom's opinion before we can take any action at all. Business stakes are high so it's best to have some backup if you get clobbered—or so the logic goes. But the plain fact is that for the most part we've murdered any useful intuitive powers we may have had in the first place. Paralysis through analysis is an all-too-common condition in the corporate world. And *that's* a slow death for creativity and innovation.

> *Intuition: 1. The act or faculty of knowing without the use of rational processes: immediate cognition. 2. Acute insight.*
>
> —Webster's Dictionary

In order to improvise, we unquestioningly, openly, and intuitively accept the initiations offered to us; we trust that every initiation is well intended, well offered, useful, and rich with possibilities. Value judgments are removed in order to employ initiations fully and functionally. We activate initiations immediately, acting on them in this moment right now. These principles build trust among our fellow players. The players act on and continue to offer initiations with good spirit, and employ these actions and offer more opportunities back to the center of the group and the central activity. We move forward *together*.

The initiation arrives in the present and, as trustworthy improvisers, we act on it now. In order to act on the initiation in the present, we must trust the moment, ourselves, our fellow players, and the environment around us. In order to act, we trust ourselves to act. We employ our intuition to act on the initiation. We feel something about the idea and we amplify on the activity using our intuitive/emotional responses. There is no other way: We move, we act, we explore, we initiate, and add and agree.

If you stop to analyze the initiation, you are no longer improvising. You're stopping, analyzing, hesitating, equivocating, or as we call it in the Comedy World, you're blocking. Blocking is the end of improvising, the end of current activity. Blocking stops forward motion, ending productivity.

To improvise correctly, you trust your intuitive self to act on the initiation, moving it forward toward new activity. You let go of the pier and float in the water. Ultimately, trust is a fragile tool—you've got to have it to start the creativity engine, but it can also evaporate all too quickly.

REPETITION BUILDS TRUST

The repetition of intuitive exercises and the reinforcement of principles not only builds trust in your ensemble/team, but more important, *it builds trust in your own intuition!* As you and your group improvise with more frequency, the ability to tap into intuition and *trust your intuition* becomes greater and greater. The value of this trust cannot be overstated—idea generators are players who are always in action, in constant development, in continuous motion. Idea artists don't worry about logical limits— they stretch, avoid, or ignore restrictions and constraints and they bend operating processes to fit their needs. Great idea artists

53

and generators and great improvisers work the exercise anyway, and regardless of its perceived limitations.

In a strange quirk of the form, experienced improvisers actually enjoy perceived limitations for the very reason that they must somehow surmount them. Improv artists revel in the challenge itself, sometimes becoming disappointed when resolution actually arrives. The play is (truly) the thing.

Through this willingness to shatter forms, they not only think outside the box, they live outside it. Yet, idea artists appreciate the box—if the box didn't exist, they'd invent one just to alter it. The game is constant and continuous—this idea, this exploration, this moment to wonder, to manage, to explore.

INTUITION AS A TOOL FOR COMEDY PRODUCTION

As a producer in the comedy industry, I have a few very important jobs:

- Cast well—a great cast makes me look like a genius.
- Set achievable and consistent short-term goals.
- Maintain quality control.
- Provide security and slightly underpay people (at least I pay).

By hiring brilliant people, establishing short-term goals, and setting high standards, I seek to build "comedy/creativity engines"—people who are focused on generating and regenerating compelling comedy. By establishing practices and cultivating/allowing for substantial chaos, we request that players concentrate on tapping into their individual and collective subconscious to generate comedy. If I do my job well, I make more money; if I screw it up, I make less.

We ask that our people tap into their intuition; we demand it. I'm not trying to take your analytical research programs and value determinators away from you; far from it. You got that MBA and I want you to keep it. The idea is to allow/incorporate intuitive exercises as a toolset for many processes:

Idea creation. Radical innovation is more about emotion than it is about logic. You *feel* good ideas as much or more than you *think* about them. Great ideas occur by tapping into the morass that is your subconscious. Sudden "inspiration," the lightning bolt that hits you with a good idea attached, is the process of your intuition suddenly opening up. This act is *immediate cognition*—knowledge suddenly gained. Improv is a device to open the intuition and achieve active knowledge.

Solution generation. Problems that defy logical solutions by definition need answers that come from somewhere else. Musing, considering, meditating, and ruminating are self-directed forms of improvisation and intuition.

Brainstorming. As individuals work together more in small groups, the group forms its own collective consciousness. Individual players' intuition gravitates toward shared visions and perceptions. Players access each other on deeper levels of communication. (This is the basis for ensemble acting, military squads, and sports teams, among many examples.)

INVEST IN INTUITION

There's a basic but potentially deadly conundrum in the business world: Managers view acts of idea generation (brainstorming, considering, ruminating, etc.) as a waste of production time and money. "Let's get to the point. What's the solution? Who's got the answer?" These demands are basic lines of dialogue in business scripting.

For anyone involved in the management of creative processes, idea generation, strategy work, or solution seeking, the practice of arbitrarily eliminating consideration time will ultimately destroy *every* functional creative process. If you ask for results before sufficient time is given to achieve useful results, you mortally damage the very function you are trying to fulfill. If this practice continues, every creative process will fail. You have my word on it.

"This can't be true," I hear you intone. "What about TV shows where the creative process has continual time limitations?" Yes, that is true. But the TV production industry depends on an unending stream of fresh idea artists as the grist for the television mill. Writers move up, move on, or burn out at an alarming rate. In most businesses, we don't have the luxury of a limitless supply of talent.

TIME FOR INTUITION

The key here is to define sufficient time, project parameters, objectives, and goals—then stick to them. Achieving innovation requires investment of time, brains, ordered chaos, and sweat; if you violate the most basic time-investment rule, you kill the process and ruin the results. Moreover, future processes—the risk of creation—will be less secure because of the fear of interruption and/or arbitrary demands. Innovation demands responsibility from the manager as well as the team.

Set your schedule and stick to it. The value that you impart to the time and space of any creative process directly and unequivocally affects the end results. If the results are important, the process must be equally so.

INITIATION AND ACCEPTANCE

Initiate — to cause to begin.

—Webster's Dictionary

Throughout this book, the case will be made for acceptance — in order to improvise productively, we must accept the initiations offered to us. Acceptance promotes progressively rewarding activity, provides permission to challenge all players, and leads us to acting on our intuition. Fully half of the results of improv interactions are determined by our ability to accept the initiation, ideas, and activities offered to us. This is the harder half for most of us because we're used to talking more than listening. The other half of the improv process is based on just the opposite ability: our willingness to initiate — to create and offer an initiation on which others may act.

All improvisers must initiate; everyone must start action when it's their turn or as the chaos of the game demands. Each individual is required to embody the activity regardless of her status, reluctance, vulnerability, or other rationalizations.

Improv affords us the overwhelmingly valuable opportunity to practice *intuitive risks* as opposed to the calculated risks we've been taught to trust. Again the battle between logic and emotion, analysis and intuition, rears its ugly head. Discomfort is a catalyst for new behavior and true innovation. Give yourself permission; allow yourself to be uncomfortable.

JOE'S RULE

Everyone must play! If you're in the room, join the game. The function of the game is to play; play is intended, by definition, to be inclusive. So play.

There are endless rationalizations to delay play: "I'm uncomfortable." "I need to understand the rules." "I like to see it work and then I'll join in." These evasions, while seeming reasonable, just delay the working/learning process. Regardless of their accuracy or truth, they don't matter to the activity or results of the work so they should be eradicated.

Accept the risk, start the game at the start of the game— even if you feel awkward or unknowing. Truly brilliant improvisation, dynamic risk-taking, is fostered when action begins without reservation. Train yourself to *jump* at the improvortunity. As improv guru Del Close said, "Fall. Figure out what to do on the way down."

A RESPONSIBILITY TO INITIATE

You must initiate. When your turn arrives in an exercise or game, begin action. Rid yourself of the internal notions of good and bad. Simply begin action. Then initiate again and again. The repetition of the act of offering builds faster, more functional offerings, but more important, it builds internal trust in your intuitive capabilities: You offer more and the offerings you offer become more functional (try saying *that* three times quickly).

As improvisers play more, they begin to accept initiations on deeper intuitive levels. Fellow players begin to feel, to subconsciously know, when you're offering something sincerely useful, an active creation immediately in this moment. When your fellow players see you truly immersing yourself in activity, without judgment or reservation, and see you unreservedly offering the word, the sentence, the idea, the song, the mood, the color, or whatever the case may be, they build empathy and understanding for you. They recognize the risk you're taking and they develop appreciation for your work. They begin to trust you and they will return trust to you. This is the fundamental nature of improv as a group creative process; it is the universal truth of improvisation.

P.S.: They don't have to like you and you don't have to like them in order to develop trust in initiations. Mutual admiration isn't a necessary component of trust. Ask anyone who's ever served in the military or had teen-aged kids. People, however, do naturally grow closer as they recognize and develop trust in each other. It's just human nature.

RISK

Improvisation demands risk. In order to contribute to any process, you have to open your mouth or move your feet, jump up and down, or do another similarly awkward activity. Do it. Commit to the activity unreservedly; eliminate your inabilities; move with compunction and commitment; act and react. As you build your risk-abilities, risk-comfort increases — players become more comfortable with risk as they risk more frequently. This is an axiomatic improv law and the energy drink of the improv player.

Improv players crave the adrenaline rush of trying something truly exotic, on the edge of their comfort zones. Great improvisers relish the buzz of risk/reward activities. They revel in risk rewarded and they take comfort in risk that fails. *At least they were out there, giving it their best shot.* This is the logic of the player and it's a powerfully addictive one.

BEGIN WITH A USEFUL SPIRIT OF INITIATION

You must *want* your initiations to be good, if they're to be useful to you and the group. Your emotional state must be productive, hopeful, energetic, directed, and active in order to initiate usefully. You must begin with a *positive attitude, an attitude on the sunny side of the street.* No matter how many times we've heard it, it still remains true. *You have to want to be good to become good.*

So, when starting an activity or initiating in the context of a process, *you have to want your idea to be good!* In the reality of the game, it may or may not be useful; *but you must implicitly and explicitly want this idea/moment/activity to be the greatest thing you've ever said and ever done!* Imagine this: *Every idea* that you initiate must have your best, hardest-working intentions behind it. Every moment of your contributions must have your most earnest desires supporting it. Every response you give to all actions must be the finest moment you have in you.

This may seem commonsensical to you—try to be good and you'll become better. But it's more than that. Most people start ideas and initiations with pretty lame desires or goals: "I'll just toss this out there. Uhm, what about this? How about. . . ." The overwhelming energy of these assertions is enough to induce sleep. Your player responsibility is to imbue your initiations with a strong desire, an energy of usefulness, excitement, pulsation.

In performance improvisation, this state of concentrated positive desire is actually somewhat easy to achieve. Your fellow players surround you; an audience waits expectedly in front of you; the lights are up, and the place is ready for good action. These conditions quicken the pulse on their own. It's easy to want to be good when everyone else is hoping you will be.

It's sometimes harder to achieve positive concentration in rehearsal or workshop environments. The pressure is off so we can coast a bit. This is when good leaders keep the standards high for everyone involved in every activity.

When players toss an initiation out to the center of the group with no commitment, the motive is, "Well, I'll just say something. . . ." Simply put, filling the air with useless words you yourself don't even believe in wastes not only your time but also the good nature and valuable investments of your fellow players. Simply put, if you want other players to care about your initiations, you must care for your initiations first. Try beginning an exercise or session with the notion, "This time, I'm going to be great! I'm going to develop the best initiations ever! My ideas will surprise everyone, even me!" Like any other endeavor, if you think you can, the possibility exists. If you think you can't, you're already right.

CHAPTER 6

Improv 101

INTRODUCTION

In order to improvise on a wide, readily accessible scale, you must first improvise in smaller, specific ranges. As you'll learn here, beginning-level games are intentionally straightforward and almost preposterously easy—in fact, you might question the purpose of the games precisely because they are so simple. But, don't be mistaken. Just as a seasoned musician returns to note scales, the greatest improvisers continually return to the simplest games to hone and refresh their skills.

Follow the activities in *Improv 101* closely for the first several times you play with your group. By the very nature of improv, no two games will play the same way twice—so repetition won't diminish the value of exploration. On the contrary, repeating the same game several times will encourage players to seek new directions. Boredom with an exercise becomes a useful tool, as well as a challenge, when the games become familiar. It's important for group to accept and understand boredom; the operating rule must be to challenge each other by continually pushing limits.

It's not sufficient to say "Agree with and fully explore every idea offered by the group": Improv practitioners must continually practice this rule themselves, embedding it in continuous activity in order to live it. The act of agreement leads to continual exploration of new concepts, activities, and directions. Accepting the challenge builds a dynamic new gateway to innovation. Insecurity, fear, and hesitancy are obstacles for improv. In order to overcome fear, we practice our skills and applications consistently, and then constantly.

WHAT I LEARNED FROM "HOMER SIMPSON"

Many years ago, Dan Castellanetta—the voice of Homer Simpson and one of the best improvisers in the world—and I were hired on the same day, into the same improv company. Dan's improvability, from the very beginning, was almost eerily brilliant. He had the brains and confidence to make choices, even at a very early improv age, that would lead scenes in extraordinary directions. Dan had the tenacity, endurance, and *chutzpah* to make interesting choices instead of obvious grabs. He resisted the mundane; he gravitated toward challenges.

By his example and generosity Dan made me a better improviser. Better players, after all, make better players. But, ultimately, it's the improviser's choice from the start to do something interesting or to make something interesting. It's not only within one's power; it's one's responsibility.

IMPROVE = IMPROV

Welcome to your first day in improv class. Here, you'll go through exercise descriptions, guidelines, goals, and the rules of the road. The lesson plan is laid out in chronological order, step-by-step. This workshop is an excellent start to improvising; yet we're not attempting to be comprehensive. As you'll see in your pursuit of improv-art, there are many schools of study and interpretations of the form. The immediate objective in this class is to get you and your group up and improv-moving.

Again, in our weird world of intuitive action, spontaneity must be practiced. This might sound oxymoronic, but it isn't. By placing one's player-self in exercises with defined forms but undetermined results, we build the skill of spontaneous initiation, of "thinking on your feet" and, more important, of acting on useful directions. Even with a deep and profound theoretical understanding of improv, there is no substitute for doing it, then doing it again. The more a player plays, the better every facet of the work becomes.

Just as the exercises themselves bear repeating, so do these facts:

- Immersing yourself in the exercise not only allows you to understand a specific application and result, but each repetition increases your ability to cross over into improv-state — the innate ability to improvise quickly, responsively, effectively, and with a sense of humor and fun. Sharpen the blade of spontaneity and it will serve you well. More play makes the player a less dull boy or girl.
- Skill building at the very basic levels increases improv talents across the range of all exercises and applications. The freedom you find early on eases the tensions of future discoveries.

Through repetition of exercises, you're not simply building skills—you're building a path to access those skills.

And now players, it's time to move on to Improv 101—the first lesson of improvisation.

STUFF TO KNOW AND DO AS YOU BEGIN

- *Form your improv group*. This lesson is designed for an inter-active ensemble. You'll need at least two or more players to get it right; ensembles of five each are the perfect size. Designate one person the leader for the first lesson; alternate leaders for each future lesson. (It's important to delegate participation, leading, coaching, and organizing equally through all workshops.) The leader will start and stop the exercises, call for breaks in the session, and so forth.

    The goal of each lesson is to build casts/teams/ensembles of players/creators who immerse themselves in improvisa-tion first for the sheer experiential fun of development. Later we want the team to target its improv skills toward specific purposes.

- *Everyone plays*. Everyone should play each game. Take turns, rotate partners, share experiences with the group— but no one stands outside the process as an observer. It's not possible to "risk half way." Do it right or don't do it at all.

- *Allow sufficient time*. A typical workshop should last at least an hour. Ninety minutes is ideal for new players. For profes-sional improvisers, two-and-a-half hours is the rough norm. This lesson is designed and timed for two hours. Players' rate of absorption will determine the duration.

- *Games have their time.* There's a distinct energy to each game. But it's virtually certain, in the beginning, that players will quit the game too soon rather than let it go too long. As the ensemble develops, leaders will feel an energy curve to each game and exercise (it's very clear and powerful in advanced groups), but in the beginning, allow for more time than less, unless the rules specifically ask you not to. It's rare that any game will take less than five or six minutes to play.

  It's also useful to allow (and, on occasion, sometimes force) a game to continue even after it seems that the ensemble's energy has faded. You'll be surprised at how much valuable work happens in these moments.

- *Listen with your heart.* Committed, *passionate* listening is the most important quality of any good ensemble. Each member of the team must listen to the group and *feel* what's being said. It's not enough to hear it, you must feel it as well. It's the natural law of improvisation and team management: Teams that don't listen will fail.

- *Feed the group ego, not the individual.* It's also critically important that individuals be able to subsume their egos to the needs of the group. The collective intelligence and consciousness of a group is greater than any individual in it. We must free ourselves from personal preconceptions in order to tap into the larger mind. It's not enough to merely accept other players' contributions; *we must value them as more important than our own.*

- *Give it time.* Building communication skills isn't easy. Like any worthy pursuit, it takes time, study, application, and sometimes money. (Bribes help.) In Improv 101, we begin at the beginning.

WARM-UP EXERCISES

Warm-ups are specifically intended to physically agitate the thought-cycle of players and groups. In the warm-up phase, we engage in intentionally "weird" behaviors to remove our sense of propriety, and free ourselves to risk and release and reduce inhibitions. We move away from logic (*thinking about what we should do*) into intuitive emotion (*feeling something and taking action on it*). Discomfort in the warm-up phase is not only useful but also actively encouraged.

One more thing: In the warm-ups, games, and challenges throughout this chapter, I'm talking to *you*, the leader. Okay, enough talk. Let's play.

"SNAPS"

- *Composition:* Group of four or more, each of which includes a leader and players, standing in a loose circle, facing center.
- *Action:*
  - Begin by snapping your fingers once upward, toward your shoulder. Then snap your fingers again in a downward motion, "throwing" that finger snap to a different player in the group.
  - Player 2 "catches" the snap by snapping her own fingers in an upward motion, then "throws" the snap to a different player in the group.
  - Player 3 catches the snap, then passes it on, and so on, with each player choosing to which other play to throw the next snap.
  - The exercise continues until you call the game to a conclusion (see next page).

- *Concentration:* Get the players to *play!* Shut out everything except the game. Allow for chat; allow for fun. Support creative snaps. Accept "mistakes" and variations as long as the group continues concentration on the game and specific activity.
- *Variation:* As the group achieves competence and comfort with the game, sidecoach variations on the central action by suggesting alternatives, which may include:
  - "Move the snap faster around the group."
  - "Alternate pace—fast then slow."
  - "Try a different rhythm."
- *Conclusion:* As the group achieves competence with the exercise, and after it's explored variations on the central exercise, call the game to a conclusion with an affirming action: "Give yourselves a round of applause," or a similar active closure.

JOE'S ADDITIONAL THOUGHTS

Definite closure to every exercise is vital for the successful management of any group activity. More important, your transition from closure of one activity, including your affirming thoughts and directions, and smooth segue to the next exercise can determine the emotional commitment of the ensemble. In improv, the players and group are at risk—they're making something out of nothing and that can be scary. When leaders act with responsibility and manage with speedy, clear dedication, players respond productively. Your function as leader is to serve the group by freeing it from any decisions other than those within the context of the exercise or game.

"SNAPS VARIATIONS"

- *Composition:* The same as in "Snaps"—group of four or more in a loose circle, facing center.
- *Action:* Begin the "Snaps" exercise over again. Let the group know that you'll be changing the context of the action as the game proceeds by talking over the action; if possible, the group should incorporate the changes seamlessly without stopping the action.

  As the snaps move around the circle and the group establishes pace and comfort once again, vary the action by applying different qualities to the snap, for example:

- "The snap is now a feather."

  Allow the group to discover the movement and action of the snap as if it were a feather—slow, light, floating between the catchers and throwers. Have the players continue the action of the finger snaps: upward motion and click when catching, downward toss when throwing. If this specific action mutates, however, allow the mutation, as well. The idea is to continue the activity while allowing for new discoveries from the players. Allow these discoveries to interact for some time. (In other words, *force the group to play, accept, heighten, and explore.*)

- "The snap is now a Frisbee."

  Allow the group to discover the new possible actions as the snap becomes a Frisbee. Keep the action flowing around the group. Support and affirm the risks it takes. As something inventive or funny occurs, recognize and affirm it. Your job is to accept and support new discoveries.

Other qualities to the snaps may include:
- "The snap is now a balloon."
- "The snap is now a bowling ball."
- "The snap is now a live rat."
- "The snap is now a boomerang."
- "The snap is now a Slinky."

- *Variation:* The entire game is continuous variation. Allow each discovery to embed itself in the group activity. Listen for laughter and "one-upsmanship" in the discovery process. These are just a few of the ideas. Add your own variations as the group advances, especially early in the formation of groups. Allow the group to find comfort in the activity, but not too much. As it experiences the shared delight of discovery and balances that discovery around the group, move on to new challenges.

- *Conclusion:* The premise and operating mechanisms are simple: Shared activity that promotes low-level creative risk-taking; transform the activity to advance new risks; allow and support the fun of exploration; require innovation to achieve simple results; force the activity past immediate unease or value judgment. *Remember, the activity is the action. Remove anything that does not support the action. This is innovation in progress. This is making something of nothing. This is creativity.*

"Hands in Circles"

- *Composition:* Groups of five or more, each of which includes a leader and players, standing in a loose circle, facing center. Individual players offer one hand to each neighbor on either side—the palm of one hand facing up, the other hand facing

71

down. Individuals connect the circle by placing their hands in the corresponding position: palm down against their neighbor's upturned palm.

Joe's Other Additional Thoughts

Humans are resistant to change, suspicious or fearful of risk. This is especially pronounced in business where risk can lead to loss. In the ongoing mastery of my work, I demand that people risk activity, discovery, foolishness, play, and more in the context of my workshops and seminars. I use every facet of my authority and expertise to require that people risk, and they do risk, willingly and openly. I've had everyone from CEOs of multinational conglomerates to world-renowned physicians to entire ad agencies risking equally across their organizations. (We once had 4,000 sales associates singing "Twist and Shout" at the same time.) The weight of the leader's authority, competence, and preparation determines whether the group will risk. If it risks, it moves. If it moves, it changes its behavior. If it changes its behavior, it learns. This is the most we can ask of anyone.

As important to the development of the group is our progressive growth as leaders. Improvisation is the art of change. As leaders, we invest ourselves in the operating mechanism of transformation *as* we direct our groups, in other words, as the group improvises, so do we. Allow yourself to discover new impetus, variation, requests, and demands even as workshops progress. Keep your plan loose enough to incorporate current stimuli into the ongoing work.

- *Action:* One person taps the hand of the person next to them and that player passes the tap to the next and so on around the group. Coach the group to keep the pace consistent. See if it can find common rhythm and tempo. Allow the game to run for some time before adding variations—four minutes at least.

- *Variation 1:* Get the tap moving around the circle as fast as possible. Force the focus of the action on the group. Make it work to move the tap faster. Then alternate to a slow, even pace.

- *Variation 2:* Stop the action. Have the group select a game leader by randomly pointing at someone in the group. (People will point in several directions. Have them arbitrarily agree on a game leader.) This new leader starts the game over, passing the tap around the group. As the first tap gets about halfway around the group, the leader should add a second tap to follow the first. Force the players' focus on the individual taps. Encourage them to concentrate on each action and then pass it on.

- *Variation 3:* If the group is large enough (nine or more players) try to get three taps going at the same time. You may also combine two smaller groups for this game. Force the players' focus on the action. Keep their concentration inward, toward the center of the group.

- *Variation 4:* Try two or three taps with all players' eyes closed. (Actually the game is much easier when players close their eyes. Visually tracking specific taps slows reaction times.)

- *Conclusion:* Allow the players to experience success and fun with this game. The concentration level is necessarily high. A tension to achieve and succeed grows with the game. Support this tension. Encourage the group to play through it.

JOE'S LEADER NOTES

At the conclusion of "Hands in Circles," again encourage the players to risk. For new groups explain that discomfort is great! *An uncomfortable feeling is exactly the state we seek!* As related in other chapters, "same old, same old" means no stretching, no movement, no growth. Only through the unusual will we reach the different, the new, the better, the odd, the radical, the dynamic. We *must destroy the box* and think outside the remnants. Warm-up games physically force us outside our comfort zones and this is exactly where we want to go—outside our norms.

Improv is a mechanism to encourage and manage change. In order for improv to work, people must change. Share this theory out loud: "If you're feeling awkward or uncomfortable— great! Now we're getting somewhere! If you're still feeling normal and safe, we'll fix that soon." The leader's job is to shake players' snow-globes and demand that the flakes float in new directions. The group's job is to accept this mission and become uncomfortable. Permission to change is granted.

"MOVEMENT IN CIRCLES"

- *Composition:* Groups of five to ten, including a leader and players, composed in a loose circle, facing center.
- *Action:* Have the group select a new exercise leader by randomly pointing to a new player. The new leader will create a simple sound (example: *woooooo*) and, simultaneously, a simple motion toward the center of the circle (example: step forward and bow). After the leader's action, the rest of the

group will imitate the sound and motion toward the center of the circle.

After the group repeats the action, the leader initiates a new sound and motion. The group repeats this one, as well.

After a third sound-motion and group repeat, the leader will point to a new exercise leader who generates three of his own actions with the group, repeating each one. The exercise leadership alternates around the group until everyone has led the game.

- *Variation:* As with many games, "Movement in Circles" is an exercise in transformation. Each person should be initiating new and different things at each action opportunity. There's not much need for variation unless players fail to risk new action. In that case, extend the turns from three per leader to a random number. This will eliminate the predictability of the game.

- *Conclusion:* Allow players (and yourself) to feel foolish and goofy. Altering, sometimes shattering, their images of "who they are" and "what they should be doing" is exactly the intended effect and function of this type of transformational game. Especially in the business world, physical activities can be extraordinarily freeing for many people. Skewing perceptions of propriety and "normal" behavior promotes risk-taking across groups and through organizations.

"TRADING PLACES"

- *Leader note:* In early stage warm-ups, we've worked smaller groups through transformational interactions specifically to get them "out of their heads." In the "Trading Places" series, if you're leading several smaller groups, combine them back into a single large group.

- *Action:* Direct players to get as far away from each other as possible without leaving the workshop space. Have players check their personal spaces by extending their arms outward, making certain they can't touch anyone close to them.

  Once players have achieved separation, have them make contact with a player *as far away from them in the space as possible.* On your cue—"Trade places"—have them trade places with that other player.

  It may be that the player they've selected is not trading places with them—the other player may have been looking at someone else. Assure players this is fine, to just travel to the new space. Once players have arrived at the new space, have them again select a player and location as far away from their current space as possible. Direct them—on your cue—to trade places once again.

- *Variation #1:* Once players move to the new space, let them know they're going to trade places again, but this time, as they move to the new space, they are to *keep as far away from other players as physically possible.* When they move toward the new space, they should keep a circle of distance around them that no other player can or should violate. This coaching directive should force them into odd movements and challenging paths to avoid contact while getting to their new spaces. Repeat this "keep-away" game several times.

- *Variation #2:* As before, players select someone as far away from them as possible. Now, however, in order to move to the new place they must be touching or in physical contact with another player.

Again, because different players will naturally have different destinations, this directive will cause all sorts of unusual movements: hands reaching across to help other players, teams of players combining resources to move together, and so on. It's an indoor version of a team ropes game. Encourage creative thinking and point out useful results.

- *Variation #3:* Have players change their emotional state while they change places. Some options: "Hurry there; be forceful this time; sneak to the next place; move backward, and so on.

- *Variation #4:* This time, as players move to the new spaces, have them get there—safely, slowly, calmly—with their eyes closed. Direct them to keep their hands up in front of them, sense where other players are, move slowly and cautiously, but get to the new space. It may help, for beginning groups or unusual venues, to have players close eyes for three steps, open them and check around, and close eyes again for three steps. Continue until players get to their new spaces.

IMPORTANT NOTE

Caution players to take care of and be safe with each other when they play games. There is an important balance between achieving an individual objective and respecting fellow players as the game is in play. Running down a fellow player in an attempt to achieve a goal violates the function of the game. Improvisation is discovering paths while supporting players; through support, we're led to new paths.

- *Conclusion:* We want players to learn to "find their way" employing new devices, options, and possibilities. These variations stimulate a controlled state of chaos among groups: individual players achieving new goals while playing with and respecting the actions of others. These traits are the basis for ensemble work. When players play well, and achieve new results in the context of controlled group chaos, we're approaching excellent ensemble development.

LET'S TAKE A BREATHER FOR REINFORCEMENT

Let's take a moment in our class to reinforce the reasons why we're doing what we're doing. It's a good idea to initiate group conversation to determine what effects and consequences the games are causing for the players. Here are some of the reactions you'll find the games will have on a group:

- Challenge players' assumptions regarding group interactions.

    Unusual physical activity in the context of group dynamics changes peoples' perceptions about what can and should happen within the group. Because we've flattened authority and hierarchy (everyone has to play), we've also abandoned normal operating procedures.
- Direct focus on individual players in the group—and the group itself—as idea resources.

    Exercises demand individual risk within a newly developed group support system. Risk/reward is reduced to simple, direct activity. Players build empathy for one another as they see one another take risks: Everyone feels equally foolish and equally successful at similar times. No genius can exist without the willing possibility (and almost certain probability) of foolishness.

- Build skills in spontaneity, responsiveness, and "being in the moment."

Virtually every exercise in the science of improvisation is a study in managed spontaneity. The rules demand activity without knowing the end result of that activity—the definition of spontaneity. Immediately responding to new initiations builds your spontaneity skills.

- Refine the ability to reach out to the group for solutions to problems.

Initiation → response → heightening → exploration = achievement. The repetition of this formula increases a player's ability to access other players for solutions to specific problems. "Giving yourself up to the group" is sometimes the best way to find solutions to problems inside and outside your personal sphere.

- Shape intuition and subconscious abilities in interactions.

As players play within group exercises, subconscious bonds—empathy, sympathy, attraction, interest, frustration—are inevitably established. As the group matures, the subconscious bonds strengthen and broaden, allowing for greater risks/rewards. At the pinnacle of excellent group interactions, stunning achievements occur: world championships, space exploration, medical advances, great comedy, and explosive monetary gain, among other things.

Personality Types

There are several personality types for which leaders should be on watch. These include:

- *The Directors.* They try to retain their personal authority or expertise by overtly steering games or directing the group from within the game itself.
- *The Meek.* They'll back away from initiations through "shyness"—a perceived inability to assert themselves, especially in front of peers.
- *The Skeptics.* They implicitly retain subtle superiority over others (usually caused by insecurity) by holding back or even subverting games or rules.
- *The Bosses.* They stand away from activity for fear of losing their status within the group.
- *The Inquirers.* They'll hesitate or fully halt activity until a series of detailed questions are answered.

Like anything that deals with human nature and personal growth, individual improv players will have radically varying levels of acceptance and absorption. It's important to note that the percentage of people who *resist* improv-change is far larger than the percentage of people who *can't* change.

Novice players defy improv-learning for the same reasons humans resist change: fear of the unknown, insecurity, loss of perceived status or knowledge, and many other subjective concerns. And while these emotions are normal, even understandable, *they are not relevant to the process!* Exercises don't care if players are nervous or shy; games don't judge you; innovation doesn't care how you access it. The end results of creative productivity don't give a hoot how you got there—you just have to get there.

Remember, improvisation is a path—take it or don't. But if you do choose to take it, boldly go where no one has gone before.

- Establish the power of group interactivity.

  A key component to building an excellent ensemble is submerging individual players' goals to those of the group. There's a dual balance to navigate here: On the one hand, it's important for players to bring their best initiations to the game; on the other hand, the frequency of initiations *must* be relatively equal among the players.

DON'T TAKE "NO"
FOR AN ANSWER

Leaders and group members: Persist in your efforts to bring the "resisters" with you. In group dynamics, there's a tendency to allow resistant players to fade back or fall out of the processes. The implicit logic is, "Well, they don't want to do it anyway, so let them out of it." Toss this perception out the window. Skeptics, shy types, and insecure players are not only valuable to the improv process—they're absolutely necessary.

From skepticism we get perspective; from shyness we get empathy; from insecurity we get awareness. The power of the group comes from the players—the individual and collective personae. The wider and more varied the individual perspectives, the greater possibilities for input and initiation.

To achieve full involvement from even the most resistant players:

- *Be persistent.* Be steady and good-humored in your encouragement of individual players. Cajole them into participation. Firm yet gentle coaching—*play the game, move into the activity, focus on the moment*—leads players away from insecurity and inaction toward experience and growth.

81

- *Encourage self-reliance.* Urge players to find solutions for themselves. As a leader, it's your job to lay out the rules and coach the players to play. You can't, nor should you try to, play the games for them. Let players know that, other than the very few rules inherent in each game, *there is no wrong way to play the game.* The rules exist only to allow everyone to participate in a game that is understandable. Once the basics are agreed to, everything else is acceptable. It's their job to play the game—a short-term, concentrated exercise in creative activity.

- *Allow fun to happen.* Let them know that foolishness is not only accepted but also *actively encouraged.* This isn't rocket science. (It's much harder than that.) Genius comes from readiness and willingness to risk looking foolish. Conversely, the player that doesn't initiate due to insecurity will never reach for innovation. You must guide players to destroy the box and feel something outside the remnants. Forget logic; let's play.

- *Play with them one-on-one.* When players are so locked up and frozen that they can't move, take them aside and play the game with them on a small and fun scale. The authority and personal attention of the leader will relieve many levels of fear.

- *Suspend judgment.* Improvisation is activity—persistent and consistent movement toward the future and the unknown. Judgment slows and stops forward movement, causing people to stop activity to review what's already past. Judgment is not a bad thing; it just can't be done at the same time as creation. The games reinforce forward, future action.

- *Expose players to vastly different situations and circumstances.* There is no substitute for "new." People who experience dynamically new activities and stimuli together form unique bonds from the experience. Life is full of these radical experiences: a group of people stuck in an elevator, stranded on a train, helping someone in a car accident. In improv, we cultivate ensembles by exposing them to risk—performing in front of each other or in front of an audience. These can be catalyzing, sometimes breath-taking experiences. Few people soon forget them. Performance of improv exercises, especially in front of peers or a general audience, melds players together through the heat of risk under stress and/or scrutiny.

- *Instigate fun.* Improvisation, at its best, is literally thrilling. It is the convergence of your inspired initiation and a fellow player's unique acceptance, both players moving forward into discovery, the ensemble following and initiating and moving forward again. Words take on new meanings, minor actions become focused and important, ideas occur in rushes of new activity, on and on.

As important as the thrill of discovery, improvisation *must be fun.* Promoting a personal sense of humor in group activities frees fellow players to have more fun. It's important that the humor support activity rather than subvert it—but it's even more important to place yourself in a conscious state of enjoying yourself.

Players should begin everything—game, exercise, warm-up, creative task, and group challenge—with the explicit intention of having fun in the activity. You may need to remind yourself and each other, but start everything with the joy of discovery and the fun of the unknown.

Through persistent applications of the games and adhering to uniformity of rules and risks, virtually all players will move toward the center of the group and activity. It will take time and patience, but eventually they'll warm to the action.

FOCUS, PLEASE

When small groups are performing for the larger group, demonstrating a game or showing progress, direct the other players watching the action to "be an audience." Their responsibilities as an audience are to give full attention, support the performing players, respond positively to initiations, add to the process when requested, and so on. Let the audience know that they'll be performing soon too. Practice the audience Golden Rule: Treat the performing players as you would have them treat you.

WHERE WE ARE NOW

We have finished with the warm-up portion of our lesson. We've gotten everyone moving and taking risks. We've moved authority and hierarchy to the side. We've suspended internal and external judgment. We're risking and rewarding and we've done a bunch of weird physical activities that intentionally put us in odd places and positions. We've also gotten our hearts pumping a little, our horizons skewed a bit, and our brains stretched toward new possibilities.

We need to review the scenery we've just seen to make certain that we're reaching the proper context—to make sure that our function is meeting our intention.

So far, our job is to:

- Jar sensibilities. Shake the snow-globe and change individual and group behavior through new activities, processes, and ideas.
- Develop the willingness to seek new approaches to new situations.
- Provide guidelines for proper group interaction and direction.
- Get *everyone* up and moving.
- Demand new connections and bridges of communications between individuals and groups.
- Have fun.

Here are some of the things new players should be saying, feeling, and experiencing:

- "This is weird but fun."
- "I guess I should listen first, talk afterward."
- "I get better ideas by acting on my thoughts."
- "I never knew these guys before. They're a blast!"
- "I'm going to take more action and talk less."
- "I didn't know there was going to be so much moving around."
- "Two heads are smarter than one, although harder to shave."
- "The most important element in getting new ideas is the group I have around me."

THEATRICAL TEAMWORK

Theater is a great mechanism for creating teams because it makes demands on the individual and group that are challenging, exciting, and satisfying to fulfill. The demands of the theater, as noted below, and their solutions, can be appropriated to a lot of different, nontheatrical environments, such as business:

- *Commitment.* Actors are naturally committed to their craft; they enter the profession out of a profound need or love for it. It's not usually necessary to investigate motives or intentions: Actors want to work, play, be spoiled, and be loved (sound familiar?).
- *Specific goals.* Shows are cast with particular end results in mind. Usually it's to create great art or a lot of money (hopefully both). So even if some process or selection is flawed, the goal remains clear.
- *Time.* Rehearsal processes guarantee that attention and focus will be provided for the task at hand. Actors know that when they're in rehearsal, they must direct all their energies to the end product, no distractions allowed. (How many times have we begged for this degree of concentration in the business world?)
- *Challenge.* Each production carries its own imperatives. No matter how easy it looks, acting is extremely demanding: emotionally, physically, mentally. (Unless you've done it, you can't imagine how exhausting it is to perform eight shows a week.) So casts are constantly challenged not only to perform well, but to perform well *often*.
- *Consistency.* Actors know one another. They're thrown together quickly and must create an immediate spark. They accept this as a condition of their jobs and their careers. They build an expectation of quality and consistency from their peers. (We must require this from our group as well.)

SHIFTING FOCUS

We now move from warm-ups to Improv Challenges. These exercises shift the focus from individual skill work, releasing inhibitions and personal expression, to small group tasks. We gradually move players from "me" to "us." Group Improv Challenges are the first step in ensemble creation.

As leaders, explain to the group that these Challenges typically have one simple objective and two or three basic rules. Define the objective of each Challenge as simply as you can; let the players struggle to find and figure out mechanisms to achieve objectives. Fight the urge to overcoach the Challenges. It's vital to note that the search for solutions is more important than the solution itself. Allow, coach, and encourage players to try devices, experiment, risk, and experiment more.

CHALLENGE #1: "BIRTH ORDER"

- *Objective:* To have everyone line up in their birthday order (their individual date of birth: June 18, September 15, etc.).

- *Composition:* Combine all players into one group for this exercise. Typically, players are scattered around the room randomly. Have them begin from there.
- *Rules:* No one may use words to find their correct space. Coach the players that they may use *any other communication device,* but they may not use words to check the birth order.

  Even though this is a simple exercise, most players will try to complicate it: "Can we speak? Can we ask each other questions once we're in line?" Remind them to find their own solutions.
- *Action:* Players will form a single-file line: the birthday earliest in the year to the left (January 1), the latest in the year (December 31) to the right.
- *Variation:* This is usually an ice-breaker Challenge, done one time in the workshop. You may, in future workshops, change the rules:
  - Line up based on your position in your family.
  - Line up by height.
  - Invent your own.

The How, What, and When of Groups

Important note: Subgroups should be periodically and arbitrarily mixed up. While there are compelling reasons to form groups and retain ensemble formations, in early improv study it's more important to expose players to the widest range of initiations possible. This is done by forming, mixing, and then reforming groups frequently. It's human nature for players to form ad-hoc groups with friends or close associates but for improv-immersion purposes, we want a wider range of risk, input, and output.

That said, this "Birth Order" challenge is an excellent way to put players in random order for eventual subgroup formation. Since at the game's conclusion the players are in a straight line, I have them count off by numbers, then form subgroups for future challenges and games by finding their coordinate numbers: "Ones over here, fours over here," and so on.

CHALLENGE #2: "OUT OF THE ROOM"

- *Objective:* Each group must convince a volunteer in the group to crawl out of the room backward. (The volunteers have no idea what their task will be.)
- *Composition:* Groups of four to six. Prior to the action, have each group select a "volunteer" by randomly pointing at someone in their group. (Several people will be pointed at; have each group agree on the volunteer.) All volunteers should leave the action area, out of earshot of the following instructions.
- *Rules:* Players may not tell or show the volunteer what to do. They may only tell or show the volunteers *what not to do.* All communication devices are acceptable: words, actions, and so forth, as long as the players don't tell or show the volunteers what to do.
- *Action:* Have the volunteers brought back to the action area and begin.

Rationalizing the Rules
Players typically have huge difficulty rationalizing this game. They'll ask many questions, asking permission to do many things: "Can we talk to them? Can we tell them that we're not going to tell them what to do? Can we write instructions to them?" But you must reinforce the objective and the rules:

Get the volunteer to crawl out of the room backward. You can't tell him or show him what to do. You may only tell or show him what *not* to do.

After you've reinforced the objectives and directions, let it be up to the various groups to find their own solutions. Resist the temptation to solve problems for individual groups. Let them fail, succeed, interact, and find solutions at their own speed. This game is specifically designed to create hurdles around a very simple objective—the groups will solve the problem at their own pace.

IMPORTANT DIGRESSION

Consider this idea for a moment: The list of "don'ts" is infinite, the list of "dos" is specific. When you want people to do something, let them know what you want them to do as simply and as clearly as possible. Most times we attempt to teach by telling our players what they shouldn't do: "Don't talk over each other; don't let your partner down; don't move that way." This practice forces negative directions on a positive activity. Improv doesn't work that way. In fact, very little positive result comes from negative teaching techniques.

The way to properly lead and teach players is to direct them in forward-moving activity. Negative directions stop action, so cut them out. It's a lot easier to get the job done when players and leaders agree to move forward on an active premise. And they'll actually know when they've achieved the goal.

CHALLENGE #3: "GROUP POEMS"

- *Objective:* The group will compose a rhyming poem of eight to 12 lines.
- *Composition:* Groups of four to six. Each team should have one writing instrument and one blank sheet or tablet. As with many brainstorm or communication games, it helps to have the group form a small circle.
- *Rules:* Warn them not to use the words "bucket" or "Nantucket"—trust me on this one.
- *Action:* One player begins by writing a simple sentence on the sheet of paper, then hands the paper and pen to the next player in line. This player contributes the next sentence and then hands the evolving composition to the next player, and so on, until a poem is composed.

   Encourage players to accept the offerings that come to them. Challenge them to accept the composition as it's being created—sidecoach them not to chat the lines out loud. The function of the game is for players to accept the creation in progress, add to it and move the offering forward. Initiation/agreement/addition/acceptance—it's the stuff of innovation.

   Shifting tactics or changing strategies at a moment's notice stimulates a sense of urgency in the creative process, and also supports the notion of spontaneous activity. It's vitally important to keep players "on their toes" in active movement. If we allow more than sufficient time for creative processes, energy tends to stagnate. Pressing the time issue, periodically, enlivens the work and objectives. (Just don't be a jerk about it, okay? Leave that to me.)

That said, after slightly less than sufficient time has passed, have each group recite the resultant poems out loud for the others. Encourage creativity in the recitation.

No Poets Required

This is a basic, perfect, and pure team creativity exercise. Wonderful, sometimes startling results can be achieved from this simple game. It's also useful to note that poetry is uncomfortable for many people in the business world. Ask them to accept the discomfort—to go with it anyway. Encourage people to surmount their discomfort by using their creativity. In this game, poems can be comical, abstract, silly, fun, touching, pained, awkward, challenging, absurd, and much more.

Remind players that we're not asking them to be anything other than themselves—just more and different selves than they're used to. The permission and encouragement of creativity is much more important than the end results.

CHALLENGE #4: "GROUP PICTURES/DRAWINGS"

- *Objective:* The group will, working in concert and at the same time, compose a picture.
- *Composition:* Groups of four to six form a semicircle around a sketch pad or drawing board. Each member has a pencil, marker, crayon, or other drawing implement.
- *Rules:* Not many; the picture can be realistic, absurd, even nonsensical. Bizarre and unreal imagery is acceptable as long as it's the operating agreement of the entire group. Allow for group chat but discourage dominant players from directing the picture toward a predetermined or authority-driven con-

clusion. The idea is to allow an organic creation to evolve with the entire group, as opposed to one person directing the construction of a theme or concept.

- *Action:* Establish a theme or image for the picture: summer, blue, sweetness, and so forth. Then have everyone initiate drawing, coloring, composing, and contributing *at the same time.* The intention (as with so many improv games) is to have players initiate, contribute, accept, and continue while the work is *in progress.* Players will be tempted to stand back and view the work of others before contributing. Encourage them to work at the same time—to absorb one another's work as they contribute their own.

At the conclusion of the exercise (8 to 10 minutes) have each group share its creation with the other groups.

Listen Up
This game promotes "listening" on several levels. As opposed to listening to verbal offerings of fellow players, participants must *watch* the creation in progress, balance their contribution, and evolve the entire theme as part of the group.

Again, as with many improv games, players will insist this multiperson drawing can't (or shouldn't) be done. Convince them, through persistent action, that simultaneous drawing *can* be done and the results are sometimes amazing. We're breaking conceptions of the "usual" way of doing things and players must be encouraged, sometimes commanded, to allow for new, purposefully unusual methods and practices. Sometimes we must lead players to the new. Sometimes we must push them there. (Push as needed.)

Challenge #5: "Move a Player, Phase 1"

- *Objective:* The group will assist one player/volunteer out of the space or room. The volunteer should be the same person throughout the action and the two variations noted below.
- *Composition:* Groups of four to six.
- *Rules:* The volunteer must have his eyes closed. The group will direct the player in action and intention, through touch and verbal direction.
- *Action:* A "volunteer" randomly selected by the group will close his eyes. The group surrounds that player and assists him in leaving the space. This simple exercise has many resolutions: Some groups will simply lead the person by the hand, others will hold the players as they move. Any solution is useful as long as it satisfies the objectives of the exercise.

Touch, Trust, Teamwork

A primary rule of every improv game and exercise is to ensure the protection and safety of each player. The two "Move a Player" games entail a huge amount of trust: one player has his eyes closed while the group takes over his direction and movements. Trust among participants is not only key, it's a function of the game. The basis of trust is looking out for one another.

Quick direction: Violate any and every rule to protect the safety of a player. In addition to trust, boundaries do exist and should be noted. Because these games involve physically touching other people, care should be taken to respect personal boundaries. At no time should even a hint of sexual innuendo or harassment be acceptable. Step outside the game when necessary to secure each other.

- *Variation #1:* As before, the volunteer must have his eyes closed. However, in this instance, the group may not touch the volunteer to assist him from the space, though it may still use verbal direction.
- *Variation #2:* Once again, the volunteer's eyes are closed. This time, the group may neither touch the volunteer, nor use words to direct him. (For really advanced levels, try one more game with no sounds whatsoever. You'll be surprised at the solutions teams will attempt.)

CAN I ASK A QUESTION?

At each level of these challenges, groups will question: "Can we touch him? Can we talk to him?" Keep directions as simple and straightforward as possible. Repeat the objective and rules of the game: "Get the player out of the space. His eyes will be closed. You may not touch him in this phase." The function of this level is for groups to solve the challenge within the rules and objectives. Allow groups to seek solutions, experiment, and risk.

CHALLENGE #6: "MOVE A PLAYER, PHASE 2"

- *Objective:* Move a volunteer from the space.
- *Composition:* Groups of four to six. Once again, the volunteer should remain the same person throughout the action and variations of this challenge.
- *Action:* The group will move the player from the space. Teams will allow themselves to figure out how within the confines of the rules noted on the following page.

- *Rules:* The group must physically, yet gently and respectfully, move (as opposed to lead) the player out of the space: carry, lift, and so on. As with every game, take care to keep players/volunteers safe, healthy, and secure. (No dropping, bumping, yanking, or any other form of improv torture is acceptable.) Players/volunteers will not take any initiative to move themselves from the space.
- *Variation #1:* Same as before except the teams may not use the mode of movement that they've already used: carrying, lifting, and so on. The groups must come up with a new mode of movement.
- *Variation #2:* Everything's the same as the last two versions except that the groups must find an ever-newer mode of movement to get the volunteer out of the room. It may become obvious that this game can go on with virtually limitless permutations—that's exactly the idea.

Speak Up

Yes, teams can speak. Yes, they can plan—they can have a gabfestival of fun. Keep a small time limit on this challenge, though. The idea is to move toward group activity to resolve the challenge. Chatting in committee diminishes the willingness to act. *Always* encourage players and teams to act! You can plan, chat, posit, confer, and enjoy any other communal communication while action is occurring.

LET'S AGREE TO AGREE, SHALL WE?

Improv challenges, like improv games, have the benefit of forcing teams to achieve new results to old challenges. The repetition of games without prescribed endings builds solution-seeking as an

operating mission and method Improv games demand that players arrive at new destinations using old maps. As awareness and
skills increase, players begin to create their own maps. (And
yet, all improvisers return to the basics to sharpen the blade, so
to speak.)

Okay, I've beaten the *idea* of agreement into you. But it's important to understand that agreement is not only a useful rule for
innovation, improvisation, and creativity—*agreement is also the operating model for group creation!* Virtually everything we've done so
far is intended to introduce, insinuate, cultivate. or arbitrate
agreement into small group operations. The rules of the games
force individuals into paths where they must find agreement with
each other if the game is to be played at all. The next exercises
carry this precept far into the night.

"ONE-WORD SENTENCE"

- *Objective:* To create a moderately coherent sentence with each
  player contributing one word at a time.
- *Composition:* This exercise can be played with partners one-
  on-one, or in groups of four to six. (I've had as many as 20
  people playing this at one time. Why not? Changing the
  composition of the game changes the game, and sometimes
  that's the best thing to do.)
- *Rules:* One word per player at a time. Encourage players
  to take their time—it's a simple sentence. Keep it that
  way. Remind players to listen to each other. Eye contact from player to player can assist individuals with
  communications.
- *Action:* Select a starting player. She contributes the first word
  of the sentence, the next player adds, and so on.

"ONE-WORD STORY"

- *Objective:* A group will generate a simple story, each player contributing one word at a time.
- *Composition:* Groups of four to six in a small circle.
- *Rules:* The objective says it all. (Allow for small gaffes and stumbles, such as someone using two words, small interruptions, etc. Most players will catch and correct themselves.)
- *Action:* One player initiates a word. The player next to her adds another word. The sentence, story, and action continues upward as each player adds more in turn.

Do You Hear What I Hear?

This game includes almost every facet of basic improvisation: initiation, agreement, acceptance, exploration, continuation, and more. At its core, it's also a listening and adding game. Support the notion of listening to each other's emotions—stories are emotional at the core. Encourage players to follow, complement, and heighten the emotion of the story. It's rare, especially in the business world, that people feel free to express emotion, even as a function of communication or creativity. Stories are emotion in order. Request that players use emotion to explore the story. Give permission to players to enjoy this game—suggest enjoyment out loud. You'll be surprised how effective such an obvious proposition can be.

HYPERACTIVE LISTENING

In order to improvise, players must listen—not only to what's being said explicitly, but also to what's being intended implicitly.

Players must hear what is being felt and feel what is being said. Actors do this for a living.

Contrary to popular misunderstanding, the craft of acting is not devoted to "recreating" an emotion or moment. Rather, acting is the successful creation of a new moment right now. Actors don't repeat moments they've learned from the past—their job is to create a new experience for themselves and for the audience. Many techniques may be employed to get actors to that place, but their function remains the same.

In order to achieve this moment-to-moment experience, actors hook into themselves and each other through a wide variety of channels: sight, sound, movement, action, intuition, and more. But, perhaps the most important primary tool for an actor is the art of *listening*.

I'm not speaking of your normal level of "active listening"—clearing yourself, paying attention, body position. I'm talking about full-contact connection with your fellow player—total, absolute, and comprehensive concentration in his initiation and its emotional and logical effect on you. Listen in a way that connects you to your fellow players' intentions—implicit and explicit, conscious and subconscious—so that you move with them on several levels.

GROUP CREATIVITY

In order to melt down our perceptions of "normal" group interactivity, in order to improvise, particular elements must be present and active. There are certainly other elements that should be included for specific purposes, but these components are the minimum daily requirements for useful group innovation.

Joe's Rules for Ensemble Improvisation
1. *Listen hyperactively.*
   - *Sufficient attention and time.* There are few things more damaging to a group creative process than a player who doesn't provide adequate time to listen to the activity or needs.
   - *Listening to understand, rather than to reply.* We all face the horrible habit, through exposure or commission, of listening just long enough so *we* can say what *we* wanted to say in the first place. Get over it.
   - *Accurate emotion.* This doesn't mean you always have to be nice-nice to listen. Rather, it means that stress shouldn't kill our listening skills. If anything, stress should increase our listening capabilities.
2. *Agree.* In order for any group to create anything useful, there must be basic agreement on the *context* of the process: what we're going to do and how we're going to do it. There doesn't need to be (there *shouldn't be*) agreement on the *content or outcomes.* After all, if you're improvising, you can't predict the outcome (other than that it will be different from other outcomes).
3. *Add.* Every person who is involved in the creative improv process must contribute to the process in turn. Using "One-Word Story" as an example, each person must add a word to the story as his or her turn arrives. (Reminder: A central lesson of improv is to increase creative output without immediate regard to its value. Players must add to the stories regardless of the "good" or "bad" qualities of their initiations.) Everyone must play. Everyone must add to the process. No holdouts or wallflowers are allowed.

4. *Accept.* Individual players must accept the group improv results as at least as valuable as their own personal results. We can never allow players to say, even inside, "I've got a better idea than this one." If they have a better idea, it must be incorporated into the process. Players and leaders must continually challenge themselves to bring everything out into the process, to leave nothing in the bag.

5. *Explore.* The job of every player is to explore each initiation, every beat of the process, as fully as possible and then explore a little more. Revel in ideas, moments, activities, and games. They're the stuff of creativity.

ONE LAST NOTE ABOUT JUDGMENT

If you follow these basic rules — listen, add, agree, accept, and explore — your creative output will increase undeniably and dramatically, even if you do absolutely nothing else. These basic components are the universal rules for functional improv processes. Let it be written. Let it be done.

In theater and improvisation, we're taught that initiations — someone else's actions and ideas — are intended as offerings, even gifts from one player to another. The idea in generation, the activity in progress, is an act of generosity from another player to you. She is giving you a small phenomenon that she's created. In business and life, this is hard for us to imagine; for so long we've been taught to view ideas and actions skeptically, analytically, and/or negatively. We can't divorce ourselves from the notion that ideas are there for us to judge.

Initiations, acts of creation, are the substance of our new ideas. If we damage the substance before we've even acted on it, we kill the process before it begins. We slaughter ideas on the altar of ego or "efficiency" or some other such bull. As you accept initiations with useful energy, you train yourself to work with everything and anything. You begin to employ disparate actions and ideas for new purposes and effects. You diminish judgment and inactivity, replacing them with acceptance and active creation. This is the path of improvisation—this is how artists work, how creators create.

Finally, as you accept and employ the actions, initiations, and gifts, it's then your job to return even more of them to the players and group. The initiations do not come into existence solely or specifically for your use. It becomes your job to heighten them, add to them, and pass them forward or upward. This is the life of the artist; this is what we do. This is also what you do in business, even when you're not conscious of it.

BRAINSTORMING EXERCISE

Our lesson moved from simple improv-movement games to group challenges and now on to a team brainstorming exercise. The following game has few rules. As the basics of improv are experienced, it's useful to let players test out theories in exercises that approximate actual business scenarios.

"CREATE (AND SELL) A PRODUCT THAT CAN'T BE SOLD"

- *Objective:* To generate and sell a product that can't be sold. Some "can't be sold" product examples include: a one-tine comb, a bald toupee, or a bucket with no bottom. Groups will generate as many aspects of the product as possible: design, renderings, unique traits. Groups should also prepare a brief campaign to sell this product to the public: slogan, benefits, target market, supplementary markets.

- *Composition:* Groups of four to six. Have sketch pads, markers, and other design implements ready for use.
- *Rules:* Not many. Use improv tools to generate group results: initiate, agree, add, accept, explore.
- *Action:* Allow groups to find their way to the objective: Create and sell a product that can't be sold. (They'll ask for lots of guidance—be sparing with direction.) Encourage use of pads, colors, drawing, and imagery. Allow for five to seven minutes for the design and brainstorming phase.

  Groups will initiate in many directions, with lots of ideas tossed around. Support this activity. Encourage groups to work through several ideas before they settle on one specific direction. All activity is good activity.

  After the brainstorming/design phase wraps up, direct groups to prepare a presentation of the product to the world in general. Everyone in the group should participate in the presentation in some way. Build the pitch for fun and humor.
- *Variation:* This is virtually the same game, except that in this case, we're going to create and present products we would dearly love: a pager that makes excuses for you, a psychic PDA, a teleport-transportation button, whatever. Same rules and directions as above.

Encourage Fun
The idea is to create a product that can't be sold and then sell it to us. This logical dilemma is actually quite common in the business world—that's why we model it in improv. It helps to apply a generous sense of humor to this game. Allow it to be funny. In the business world, the fun gets sucked out of most processes quickly

enough. In this exercise, let's hold on to the fun as long as possible. Allow the presentation to be entertaining and pleasant, even raucous if possible.

CONCLUSION

It's paramount in the work of improv that individual players support other players in the group. This support extends to the specific language we intentionally use to convey our analysis of offerings. The most important value to consider in group creativity processes is to analyze rather than criticize: Analyze offerings rather than criticize results. The idea is to subjectify the creative process (make it personal; emotionally embrace creativity) but objectify the results (Does it work? Does it achieve our objectives?).

We examine the results to see if they achieve goals and objectives rather than placing personal value judgments on them. This is harder than it sounds—our world passes judgment much too easily. We must stop ourselves and our fellow players from using typical judgmental terms: "I don't like that idea." "That's a dumb idea." Or worse yet: "My idea isn't very good." "I never come up with good stuff." Simply put, we don't have time for this kind of negative action; it just kills all positive direction, so get rid of it, now.

Allow me one more moment on this subject. My rules are not intended to turn you into touchy-feely, huggy, nonjudgmental geeks. The simple concept is that by snapping our judgments we kill ideas that are not only viable, but sometimes brilliant. In improvisation, *we're not allowed to let go of ideas until they are exhausted!* Live this concept and you will become more innovative and artistic, and smarter. (Okay, we'll see about the smarter part.)

Creativity and innovation do not recognize authority and hierarchy. Ideas must come from everywhere and everyone; we must support the ability to offer, initiate, and share. We build the responsibility of creation into the player and into the group. It's everyone's duty to work the work.

Finally, in order to improvise, it's required that we move from logic into emotion. Move there and you'll become more innovative. Writers write; runners run; creators create. If you desire more innovation, become more innovative.

Here are the top 10 principles that are the basis for team communication and the creative process:

1. There is *agreement and acceptance.* Agreement is the central process by which we create all of our materials in improvisation. The basic principles of agreement are:
   - Value others' ideas more than your own.
   - Initiate as much as possible. Add within the group context.
   - Accept ideas as valuable contributions.
   - Add when you can add.
   - Explore everything and then explore a bit more.
   - Separate the creative process from the judgment process.
   - Play.
2. *Creativity is emotion.* What you feel is more important than what you think.
3. *Innovation demands investment.* Ideas must have attention, space, and time. When creativity is given time and space, it is also given value.
4. *Repetition of creative processes builds skill.* We must train teams to become creative on demand. Eliminate the notion of waiting for inspiration. Get to work and play.

5. *Improvisation is risk.* Risk must be part of the operational model, a demand of the process. Risk is not to be merely tolerated but openly embraced. "Failure" is every bit as important as success. In fact, if you're succeeding in your improv and creative processes all the time, you are not stretching yourself enough, not pushing your personal envelope past its creative boundaries. If you're succeeding all the time, you're doing something wrong—or you need to start doing something wrong. The concepts of success and failure are nowhere near as important as our improv immersion into risk and recovery.

6. *Separate judgment.* Nothing kills good ideas and positive teamwork more quickly than a faulty judgment process. Separate creativity and judgment processes so that ideas and initiatives exist before judgment is made. Teach groups to analyze rather than criticize. Form a separate list of questions that may be used in later analyses of the materials.

7. *Build a useful spirit of creation.* There is a choice to live one's life creatively by generating and sharing great offerings. Care about what you do and other people will care about what you do. Consider what you do: If it's valuable to you, it'll be valuable to others.

8. *Take responsibility.* If you expect an idea or assertion to be valued, you must value it first. True creative thought must be shared and it must be shared well. There is risk in offering but the risk must not be avoided due to personal insecurity.

9. *Become comfortable with yourself.* Stop internal negative judgments. People sense approval/disapproval more quickly than it can be stated consciously. Train yourself to open

your own mind to creative thought. After you've accomplished that, you then can manage teamwork and creativity constructively.

10. *Let the group be smarter than you.* More minds mean more ideas. Great improvisers make other people's ideas great.

Whew! Improv 101 done and done. Now repeat it as many times as necessary. Add other games and come up with new ones of your own. Afterward, you may commence with the rest of this truly brilliant theory.

Discovery versus Invention

Discovery is an exercise in possibilities. Invention is a trial by endurance.

—Joe Keefe

If I asked you to define the words *discovery* and *invention*, it's very likely that without giving it too much thought you'd define them as meaning exactly the same thing, or at least as very similar. You might even accuse me of playing a game of semantics. And while I'll admit to being a game player, I'm sitting out this round. Discovery and invention aren't the same, at least for our purposes here. They might both have attributes we'd admire and of which as improvisers we'd want to take advantage, but they are separate activities with their own qualities, and their own influences on how we act within the process of improvisation.

Understand what they mean, what they allow you to do and

109

not do, and you'll be a better improviser—and a better business person.

THE DELIGHT OF DISCOVERY, PART 1

The act of discovery is the core of improvisation. Discoveries of new activities, ideas, thoughts, forms of cooperation, themes, and directions are improvisation's operating components. If improvisation is the transportation you use to navigate intuitive and conscious roads, discoveries are the destinations and landmarks we pass along the journey. By initiating activity in concert with fellow players and taking action on intuition, you lead yourself to thrilling and compelling discoveries—unique findings that are attainable in no other way.

Discovery is current, in the present tense. Discoveries happen *now*. The properties of new discoveries are unknown and unexpected—that is, until we uncover them. Exploration of the unknown is by its very nature challenging and difficult. In improv, we expect (we even demand) to discover new things all the time.

Discovery travels light; the expectations are by their very nature unexpected, so the results are easily obtained. There are no preconceptions, so whatever results occur are joyful surprises.

Discovery is a journey and a mission, directly related to our need, as human beings, to evolve and progress. Through discovery, we acquire valuable experience, information, and education. It changes our behavior by affecting and widening our frame of reference. We are drawn to discovery, in addition to the rewards, because it becomes a skill: Good pathfinders become better pathfinders and lead those around them toward the fulfillment of important goals. Great discoverers are leaders by definition.

Discovery demands freedom of choice, movement, activity,

and direction. Because we have far fewer predetermined limitations in discovery, our scope widens; virtually everything becomes a possibility simply because we don't know what the realities *aren't* or what the end result should be. Nobody has told us we can't—so we think, maybe we can.

We must allow the moments to happen, always resisting the temptation to force moments or artificial ideas on each other or onto the process. Improv is a discovery process, a system of innovation practice. The basis of improvisation is freeing your mind of predetermined limitations and allowing your intuitive character, acting in agreement with other intuitions, to discover new activity, new direction, and unknown territory. The action of combining your intuition, through agreement, with that of others in a group context, forms a larger intuitive base for discovery. Minds merge to explore new regions.

INVENTION

The act of invention, however, assumes a predetermined result or process. You need to know what you want to invent in order to invent it. Due to its limited spontaneity, invention can become a list of can'ts or won'ts until the sheer force of effort overwhelms the search or until the investment of effort outweighs the end results.

Invention may certainly provide a sense of achievement but rarely sparks the emotional peaks of found knowledge, dynamic experience, or brilliant vision. Due to the nature of inventing, our focus becomes narrow and limited. Our direction becomes specific but static. That's why it's unfortunate that the business world leans too heavily on invention as the *sole* source of solutions. Invention, in performance terms, is relied upon too much.

111

In fact, it's almost always insincere—a counterintuitive process. Invention, in innovation terms, slows the free exchange of initiations because of its inherently narrow, limiting focus.

The results of both discovery and invention in some endeavors may mirror each other, so either process may be equally acceptable given that you may achieve something useful as the end product. But when applied in improvisation, the processes of invention and discovery are absolutely, positively mutually exclusive: *Improv leads us to discovery; invention leads us to the laboratory.*

MOVE FORWARD INTO EXPERIENCE (NOT BACK INTO MEMORY)

The urge to invent forces us backward into memory: "What do I know? What do I remember? Where is the information I need? How did we do that other thing?"

Discovery, on the other hand, leads us forward into experience: "Hey, why did that work? How did those ideas come together? What if we tried it this way?"

To improvise, we have to resist memories and instead force ourselves to go boldly . . . anywhere. Any direction, any action, every movement is better than reversion to the refuge of our past experiences. You don't need to—you can't—*deny* your past experiences; they got you here so they must be worth something.

Yet, when improvising, they're just irrelevant to the process. When improvising, you're not the sum of your past experiences; you're the sum of your present and future experiences. As an idea artist, you're only as valuable as your presence in the present and future tense: Doing, being, moving, forwarding, progressing. We'll stop to look back at the scenery when we're done.

In our comedy world, new improv practitioners try to invent "funny" all the time. Instead of trusting the usefulness of a smaller, sincere scene, they lunge toward larger, faster (usually dumber) scenes or character work. The thinking is that the more words there are, and the faster and louder they are, the funnier the scenes. Improvisers must be trained away from this impulse: Hilarious scenes, interesting dialogue, and powerful characters aren't conceived in the knee-jerk reflex of *trying* to be funny. Important comedy is found in the security of theatrical command, controlling the audience and environment, and by crafting sincere discovery. Once useful discovery occurs, pacing, timing, character amplification, and other elements can then be worked into the context of the comic moments. But discovery must be allowed to exist first. When you're improvising, move toward discovery and back away from inventing.

YOU DON'T NEED TO KNOW; YOU NEED TO DO

A common trait shared by great improvisers is their inability to explain what they did while they were doing it. Their intuitive improv engines become so powerful that they move away from reliance on consciousness—they become completely possessed by the moment and the activity around them. Great actors employ deeply defined characters to accomplish this state—they "lose themselves" in their characters. This ability is a good thing for improv artists, worthy of pursuit. As the work evolves, actors trust the characters they build. Improvisers build an internal relationship with their own intuitions: They enjoy the characters they create.

By accessing these characters, this bond with the character (while seemingly psychotic) is actually a playful way to get to know oneself better. Through play-acting, children do this naturally. They're in touch with their intuitive side because *they give priority and security to their intuitive selves.* The lessons we can learn from children, natural improvisers, are too many to list and usually hilarious.

STUFFED SHIRTS

Locked-up, stuffed-shirt types resist improvising because not only can't they cross the bridge to their own subconscious, they can't even find it on the map. They may become awkward, embarrassed, and insecure, and even ridicule the process instead of allowing their own risk-taking and vulnerability. Consider how few people in authority purposely risk appearing odd or funny or silly or foolish. The answer is almost none; we hold onto our notion of pride instead of seeking the experience of something new, odd, and wonderful right now.

FEAR OF FAILURE

The business world attaches much more emotional importance to failure than to success. "Failures" are hotter stories, carry more consequences, and have a deeper emotional impact on the audience than successes. It's a condition of business that the negative consequences (i.e., failures) of risk/failure are greater than the positive ones (i.e., rewards) of risk/success. This circumstance may be a universal law of business but for improv purposes, we must suspend this law. Discoveries come from risk. Great discoveries come from large risks.

Everything you need exists in the world directly around you. Every idea, initiation, impulse, direction, and innovation is present and within your reach. Every great idea needed to bring your company to new levels of success, through innovation, already exists within the brainpower of the organization. You already have it! You just have to learn how to access it fully.

THE DELIGHT OF DISCOVERY, PART 2

Improvisation, in comedy performance, is a shared event between the performers and the audience. The performers, their concentration occupied with the present needs of initiation and acceptance, seek and find discoveries in the improvisational execution of their art form. These discoveries are organic to the moment and environment. They exist as bubbles of experience in this exclusive here and now. The performers are immersed in the intuitive paths of their performance. Their focus is deep in the concentration of this specific event of creation. Actors feed and thrive on the occurrence of these organic opportunities. Performers find validation in moments of discovery; they experience intense moments of gratification in the fulfillment of their craft.

The audience, sensing the spontaneous power of the developing experience, delights in the shared discovery. The audience, as privileged participant, revels in the moment, subconsciously bonding with the immediate performance. This identification—the awareness of spontaneous creation—produces a unique and intense union between the audience and the players.

These phenomena—concentration leading to discovery and privileged participation in the creative process—are the "delight of discovery." The delight of discovery is the basis for live theater, comedy, and art.

PURSUIT OF DELIGHT

Comedians create jokes that amuse themselves first. Jazz improvisers demand more from themselves and their instruments. Painters, writers, dancers, video game designers, film makers, and flower arrangers push the limits of their works. They push to new levels to achieve the delight they experience in the advancement of their art form. The challenge to achieve something useful right now spurs the artist to more exploration, higher ranges of risk, better execution of forms, and ultimately, more vibrant results. This is how the performance envelope is stretched— through the intrepid pursuit of the new.

As we build connections to intuitive processes and shed the creative restrictions of logic, we gravitate toward conditions and terms that are generally excluded from business language: delight, charm, amusement, satisfaction, fun, and more. For reasons cited earlier, bizpeople are almost congenitally suspicious of these conditions. Many people simply reject or suppress the emotions themselves. Very few people in the bizworld know how to cultivate them.

In business terms, delight itself is the emotional confirmation of innovation—*people feel good ideas!* Delight is the internal manifestation, the sense of accomplishment of an idea or inspiration that is useful; it is your psyche's way of telling you you've done something good. As business managers and idea artists, we must cultivate and reward delight in our associates in order to stimulate even more and better ideas from them.

Delight, whenever possible, should be shared publicly. Good ideas become even better ideas when shared in open forums. And the personal affirmations that people receive from good ideas shared aloud are invaluable rewards for improv/innovators; acceptance provides incentives and nurtures risk-taking.

FACILITATION OF DELIGHT

Brainstorming sessions should occur in open forums. Here are some general guidelines for best results:

- Start with an improv warm-up (see Chapter 6).
- Set and post objectives for the entire group. Be clear about definitions of the objectives and individual and group responsibilities.
- Create and post schedules.
- Violate some of the rules. Keep everyone less balanced by throwing in physical exercises, challenges, etc. Ideas and innovation are activities first; keep everyone active.
- Allow time to prepare reports from subgroups.
- Challenge the reports to be as creative as the content. Encourage subgroups to be creative, entertaining, and compelling with their reporting. Do the report as a commercial, for instance, or have each person take a new role in the report, or sing the darned thing. (We're trying to delight and challenge the audience in addition to ourselves.)
- Randomly select subgroups to deliver reports. Random selection promotes more spontaneity and reduces stage fright for the nervous (they don't have a deadline looming).
- Clearly define audience/listener responsibilities. The jobs of the audience are:
  - *To listen.* This means hyperactive listening, of course. Acceptance is the second priority rule in improvising; groups are as responsible to the rule as are individuals.
  - *To empathize.* What is the subject? How can I help? What would I do with it?
  - *To initiate and add.* "I've got an idea . . . what if you . . . how about if. . . ." Synthesis of ideas raises the bar for every-

one and taps into the greater intelligence of the whole group.

- *To create an environment that allows/accepts risk and supports discovery.*

SUPPRESSION OF DELIGHT

Many great ideas have been unwittingly destroyed by an unreceptive audience. Risk-takers face enough of a challenge simply generating the idea. An unreceptive or distracted audience damages the work simply by not being ready to accept the information. In every improvisational exchange, the audience has its equal and fair share of responsibility: Be ready, be aware, pay attention, offer useful input. The abdication of this responsibility will damage the craft and diminish future work.

The suppression of delight—when people aren't allowed to have fun—carries consequences damaging to innovation. In environments of fear, anxiety, or stress, people will continue to create and innovate; but a significant portion of their energies will be devoted to employing their creativity to relieve that same fear, anxiety, and stress. Catastrophe is a prime motivator for creativity; anxiety is, too.

The simple gesture of offhandedly dismissing a heartfelt idea carries repercussions well past the moment: You're not only rejecting the idea but you're also teaching the offerer not to bring you ideas in the future. Not only is this dumb, it violates the Second Rule of Improv: Thou shalt accept. If you choose not to accept, you lose and the players around you are allowed to quit.

Arbitrary acceptance, when practiced consistently, teaches the acceptor not only to listen well but also to synthesize better ideas from the initiations offered. We must find the best in the things that are offered and make the best of them.

FIND THE BEST IN THE OFFERING

Initiate; accept; search for the best in the offering. Mel Brooks's function in life is to make *any situation funny.* He doesn't get to pick and choose what happens in life; his job is to take what's already there and turn it into funny. Ultimately, this is the responsibility of any serious humorist—to take things and make them funny. Good comedians don't wait for the funny to come to them; they go to it. They take what's in front of them and twist it, turn it around to make it work. Death, taxes, cabs, significant others, whatever the subject, there's enough there for any comic worth his or her per diem.

Our job as improvisers is to take what comes and work it better. Listen for the best in the offering, dig for it, suffer for it, but find it and work with it. *You may not reject any idea, offering, assertion, or suggestion until you've worked it over!*

CONCLUSION

Discovery leads to inspiration, which leads to further discovery, which leads to even more inspiration. The positive cycle of improv discovery builds on itself—creative momentum is generated, increased, and sustained.

Invention depends on logic, analysis, repetition, and repetition. Inspiration must occur *in spite of* the process. Through the use of improvisation, *we begin with inspiration as our operating mechanism.* Allow yourself to explore. Permit yourself to discover. Your innovation results will increase incrementally.

The Value of Failure

EMBRACE FAILURE

To improvise is to fail.

—Viola Spolin

Improvisation, at every level, demands that players challenge themselves and the improv work in order to attain drastically distinctive innovation. Music, art, writing, brainstorming, comedy, product development, and strategic planning are just a few of the areas where improv is implemented to extend the boundaries of the discipline. A fundamental application of improv is to expand the context of the form in use, to bend and stretch the accepted doctrine of each form. Through this extension ability, improv artists elevate disciplines by expanding their scope.

In order to expand their range, improvisers move outside

existing contextual barriers; they risk, create, venture, challenge, journey, explore, attempt, and improv their way to new horizons.

> *. . . . to boldly go where no one has gone before.*
> —Star Trek

An inescapable consequence of this content-stretching is the perception that the improviser is, within the common understanding of what failure means, "failing." "Failure" is assumed because the end results of the improv action deviate from the normal direction of the discipline at work. Picasso, e.e. cummings, and the Marx Brothers, for instance, were all radicals who extended their art forms through improvisation, who at one point or another "failed," though they failed "up."

Failure, and its mutating effect on forms, is the purpose of improvising in the first place. Artists accept failure as an integral part of every creative process—they *must* fail in order to achieve genuinely innovative concepts. Artists purposefully fracture process to bring about results unexpected even by themselves.

This risk-requirement forces us to reevaluate our conceptions of success and failure. *Failure must be permitted, even encouraged, into the creative/intellectual process.* Failure must be accepted as an integral component of emotional/intellectual exercise. As improv leaders, we must not only allow for failure, we must demand it.

> *If you never fail, you're not trying hard enough.*
> —Joe Keefe

> *Winning may be the only thing—but you don't start there.*
> —Me, again

Likewise, the traditional concept of success must be separated from the improv process itself. Players must be *doing it* rather than judging if they're doing it *well*. Approval, from our peers and ourselves, is an addictive ego-feeder but a useless impediment to creative action (as opposed to useful impediments that provide direction and goals). This is scary stuff for those less secure in their improvability, but the fact is that failure is reactive at best. Improvisation is active—artists must move to activity without immediate consideration of value judgments.

Writers write. I let the audience judge my shows.
—Neil Simon

REHEARSAL

Artists train themselves away from the perception that failure is a bad thing through many devices: repetition, role-playing, rehearsal, and exercise, among others. Fortunately, a good many artists were born with the considerably healthy attitude that they don't care what anyone else thinks regardless of the situation.

As artists achieve contextual excellence in their work, as they achieve mastery over their medium, they begin to demand and expect failure from themselves. They test themselves, drive themselves to creative anarchy, pushing the limits of their abilities to discover novel results. They induce failure to open their own minds.

In business, we're not allowed many failures, so innate improv skills atrophy and waste away. Yet innovation, like artwork, demands failure. In order to gain the full benefits from improvisation (and failure), we must exercise our ability to risk. We accept challenges that take failure into consideration of the end result. We allow for sufficient time to challenge ourselves in a controlled, protected environment. In other words, we rehearse. We promote and allow changes in our perspectives, directions, and actions to extend the work and the form. We initiate risk to find reward.

One of the most important attributes improvisation offers to a business person is a secure context (and a secure place) in which to risk and fail. By forcing ourselves to move into unusual and diverse directions—in a context (and place) where we're supported and secure—we find out more about what we need, what we are, and what we can do.

> *There can be no freedom without the freedom to fail.*
> —Eric Hoffer

WE AGREE IN RISK

In order to improvise usefully, improv artists must first accept the context of the exercise or endeavor. As we've noted earlier, acceptance of *content* is not absolutely necessary; in fact, sometimes it's better to ignore the content while improvising, but it's critically important to agree on *context:* the form the exercise or endeavor is taking.

Definitive goals for the exercise or process are not absolutely necessary—and again, sometimes it's desirable to ignore them, anyhow. Preplanned goals may lead us back to "normal" thinking and "regular" activity.

Acceptance, though, must go much farther than simple agreement on the rules of the game. Acceptance is a conscious willingness to let go of our preconceptions and allow ourselves to be affected by the activity and initiations around us. This is big stuff, more important than you know. Acceptance is the most difficult

concept for businesspeople to truly incorporate into their improvising. We've been taught, from our earliest education, to form
judgments, generate opinions, and create values from the information we receive. This practice of creating and experiencing
snap judgments destroys innovative action. We overlook the current, active usefulness of materials offered to us in the here and
now. We judge the results before we've even explored them and
often reject the offerings provided.

In improvising, we move to automatic acceptance of the initiation—deal with it, manage it, turn it upside down, and explore it
until the energy is gone. We toss, chat, brainstorm, and cultivate
the idea without conscious judgment. Success in improvisation is
found in the activity itself, not in the conclusion. In improv, the
activity and end results are the same thing.

ACTING IN THE PRESENT/
MASTERING THE MOMENT

The craft of acting forces the performer to stay immersed in the
moment. The craft requires actors to have deep powers of concentration and to be able to muster and direct intense energy in
specific paths with precise timing. Actors employ a wide range of
exercises to refine these powers of concentration and directed energy, some of which were illustrated in Chapter 7. These exercises and drills help refine an improviser's ability to be in the
moment, in the here and now. They help form the ability to "turn
it on" so an actor can feel immersed in an environment, current
emotion, activity, experience, and challenge.

Acting is an immediate art form—it's happening now. Actors
are immediate people—they want action now. This quality is
unusual for many in the business world, which makes it an

interesting yet exceptionally difficult trait for businesspeople to study and embody.

The mastery of the moment, immersion into present activity, is key to high-quality improvisation. Eliminating the past and ignoring the future are key areas of concentration for the improviser. Letting go of the past and letting the future be what it will frees the improviser to play with the work in front of her. Children are experts with current moments: They find play and amusement and interest in small things. They find stimulation on their own, when we let them, and they concentrate on that stimulation. They turn boredom into innovation (that's why they often like the box as much as the expensive gift that was found inside it). Children can teach us a lot about originality, if we let them.

But, I digress. Back to the point. As great improvisers, we churn "failure" into new product; this is the essence of our job, one of the purposes for which improvisation exists at all. Let's assume you're brainstorming a new slogan for an airline. In the exercise set, your group builds a list of images relating to the positive aspects of air travel: exotic, fun, adventure, scenic beauty, and so on. In this case, one of your group players misunderstood the directions and has evolved a list of images in an airplane itself: seats, food, flight attendants, air-sickness bags.

Accept the results of this "mis"direction. There are myriad ways you can marry the images to achieve the slogan exercise: *We have the most exotic seats in the air! Our food is an adventure in itself!* Whatever the results, it's important to include "mistakes" or "failure" as an integral, normal part of the process. This is acceptance and the beginning of agreement.

WE TRY TO FIX

When we think we've hit a spot of failure, most of us assume that we then need to "correct" the content, redefine the context, and backtrack over the exercise. Resist this practice. Continue on from where you are with what you have. By exercising the failure into the process, by forcing the group to accept the "abnormal" response and the usual mistakes, you not only sharpen the communal brainwork, you build in the expectation of continuing activity and forward motion, despite supposed stumbling blocks.

As you fail, accept, and then move forward, you will find surprising successes beyond any reasonable expectations. No kidding—a huge percentage of comedy comes from expectations that are unpredictably altered by the performer. They lead the audience in one direction, then they take us in another. Unexpected or altered prospects are the stuff of original thought.

For our business purposes, we want to stimulate the improv brain by embracing the unusual, the unexpected, and the plain weird.

CONFLICT

Our world is overwhelmed with conflict: personal and global, sociological and commercial. Conflict is a seemingly integral component in our culture. Yet improvisation is based in agreement and acceptance—the virtual opposites of conflict. Improv is the action of synthesizing opposing ideas or initiations. This is the rule and the operating mode of the work.

Improv demands agreement. To improvise you must listen, initiate, act, and repeat. While enacting the rules, you must accept stimuli and agree with initiations as they occur. This is where the stuffed shirts meet their match. It's sometimes impossible for some people to agree without reservation, with full commitment. In our seminars, this is where we encounter the most serious resistance to improv and its uses:

The IT person who wants to retain her silo of expertise.

The VP who can't be seen to be vulnerable.

The manager who won't risk looking dumb.

The team member who's worried about his hair.

The admin who doesn't think she's creative.

It doesn't matter if the reasons are true or valid; to improvise you must find agreement inside yourself and share it with others. Agree to risk, agree to try, agree to accept the rules, agree to fail if you have to fail; the list is infinite. Objections are conflict — emotional, personal concerns. Improvisation is productivity; if you must risk something to achieve improv, then you must risk it. Let go of the pier and float in the water. It will support your weight. It will make you buoyant.

> *Try? Do not try. There is no try, only do.*
>
> —Yoda

EMBRACE CONFUSION

You need more confusion in your thinking! You need to immerse yourself in perplexity, uncertainty, and misunderstanding. You must revel in an unknown path that leads somewhere other than where you thought it would lead. Sometimes you must shake the system, add too many ideas to the process and overwhelm your brain with information. Other times you should inundate your-self with unrelated imagery and change the path of least resis-tance to a flood of improbabilities.

Early on, we get used to the idea that confusion is bad, un-healthy, and scary and that order is logical, safe, and good. We've been taught wrong. We run from confusion like it's the plague. We reject newness simply because it's new. If we keep this up, we stay put, *in situ*, and eventually, we are simply un-able to move.

Instead, we'll move into environments less usual, more chaotic. As we roam within our creative mayhem, we unearth new posi-tions and perspectives—we live outside the box. The next group of new exercises is designed to immerse you and your group into useful states of creative chaos.

Five Exercises
1. "Confusion and Not."

    Stand in the center of a small group of three to five peo-ple. Each person in the circle will initiate an intense conver-sation with you *simultaneously*. Have them select something important or a cause they believe in for their subject. Have each person begin their chat with you. It's your job to main-tain each conversation at the same time it's happening. You must work each conversation as fully as possible, allowing confusion when it exists but fighting your way toward clar-ity. It's up to you to agree, forward the content, and keep the game moving.
2. "Random Images."

    Have a partner select five unrelated images: pictures, paintings, or drawings from several sources, such as maga-zines, newspapers, and books. Then select five images for your partner. Each of you will create an original story combining the images into one tale.

3. "Image Expert."

   In a group of three to five people, have a person select five unrelated images for you. Without previewing the images, begin a speech on a favorite subject or hobby. Incorporate the images into the story as part of the content and text of your spontaneous speech. *Avoid commenting on the randomness or inappropriateness of the images*. Your job is to incorporate the materials seamlessly by accepting them as they are and as they occur. Allow the story to evolve. Accept the images as they arrive—embrace them as valued gifts.

4. "Random Words."

   Have a partner place 10 dissimilar, unrelated words in a randomly dispersed pattern on a large piece of paper. Do the same for them. You can select the words by turning pages of a book or dictionary. Compose the sentences into a comprehensive story that links the ideas together. Again, allow the story to evolve; accept the words and their meanings.

5. "Pointing Story."

   Have a partner select a story at random from a newspaper or magazine. The partner will read it aloud, omitting each noun as it occurs. The partner will point to you to fill in the omitted word. Don't worry too much about logical context or flow. Allow the story to unfold. Try some contexts where you attempt to keep this particular story intact; try others where you incorporate disparate images. The idea is to be freer than you were before you began.

INCREASE THE AMOUNT OF IDEAS

When I'm writing a script, my wife sometimes teases me about a particular gag. "That's not a very funny joke," she'll say. I patiently explain that they don't all have to be *good* jokes; they just have to *be jokes*. A healthy and consistently large volume of comedy will overwhelm the occasional clunker. The point is, sometimes she's right, sometimes not, but it doesn't matter anyway. I'm continually training myself to write a greater volume of higher-quality jokes. As production levels increase, there's a greater selection of more refined jokes. Waiting for the one, perfect, pristine, killer comedic joke will only serve to stifle the rest of the comedy. For yourself, move toward higher production levels of ideas, even wildly confused ideas. We'll select the best ones later.

BE DRAWN TO CONFUSION; REVEL IN UNCERTAINTY

Great improvisers love danger. They not only drift toward the edge of the creative cliff, they sprint over to it. They catch a powerful adrenal buzz from the execution of their craft—being out there where even they are not sure of the direction. It's exhilarating, addictive, and a whole lot of fun.

In improv comedy, there are many times when the activity is at work, the joke in progress, the idea offered, the action taken, all before the players fully understand what they've done. Many comics will tell you that their best jokes were totally unplanned, completely out of the blue. They had no idea what they were going to do, or that the joke would be funny at all—they just did it, and it worked.

In order for "it" to work, you must accept it as is—activity and offering for its own sake and with its own value. Trust your intuition. It can lead you to new horizons.

FAIL/NOT FAIL

Seek out the chance for failure like it's an empty life raft and you're last one off the *Titanic*. Grab failure and confusion with both hands and keep them close. The art of improvisation and important creative results are fostered by two prime motivations:

1. *Nurturing:* creating an environment where risk is supported.
2. *Disaster:* when everything is melting down around you.

These are times where you simply have to be creative.

Who among us isn't attracted to the problem solver, the fixer, or the really great idea guy? We rush to these people when we're confronted with obstacles or challenges. They're the ones who know the way out, the pathfinders to safety. They're the ones who turn failure into success. We seek out these folks in times of distress or challenge. They're our mentors, our parents, our teachers, the smart guy in the office. It's considerably harder to turn ourselves into one of these people, but to become a great improv artist, we move down this path. In order to increase our creative artistry and improvability, we begin to equip ourselves with the tools to change our circumstances to fit our needs—and we also begin to build an environment that allows and inspires us to change for the better.

CHAPTER 9

Practical Applications and Actual Case Histories

INTRODUCTION

So far, we've covered some basic brilliant theory and your first improv lesson. The question lingers: *How do you apply this stuff to regular business life?*

I'm glad you asked. In this chapter, we'll cover a wide range of application examples from my company's list of corporate clients. Before applying improv techniques in a company setting, my company immerses itself in the culture and environment of our client in order to understand the conditions, circumstances, and needs of the company and its associates—we move in with them for a bit. This extensive investigation allows us to craft programs that are targeted directly to client needs.

As with any commercial consultative process, our recommendations must positively affect the environment, the culture, and ultimately, the bottom line. We respect (and greatly appreciate) the investments and relationships our clients build with us. The very least we can do is help them make more money, and have a bit more fun doing it.

Improvisation impacts business cultures at the personal and team communications level by building more effective ensembles, and providing individuals with new skills in spontaneity, idea generation, and communications. Companies that have improvability become healthier, more enjoyable, and more attractive to new associates.

Finally, we look toward improv mechanisms that will assist companies at the bottom line: applications to generate new and better innovative ideas, provide superior customer service, build excellent teams, attract more customers, lure and retain better employees, and ultimately make more money. This is the message and the mission.

The examples that follow demonstrate just a few real-life applications and results of improvisation in the business world:

MAJOR FOODS MARKETING TEAM— MORE RELISH PLEASE

Who they are:	Major food company marketing department; 80 idea-generation associates from marketing and sales disciplines.
What they do:	They market enormous quantities of packaged foods; building and extending product and brand awareness.

What they wanted: To sell more condiments. Specifically, to tie together combinations of prepared foods in unique and compelling summer takealong packages.

The Improv Focus
In our daylong workshop, we concentrated on improv applications for team idea generation. We played the product-selling game from Chapter 6, utilizing many variations to stimulate dozens of new marketing concepts. Ultimately, the teams came up with a broad variety of packaging concepts that resulted in a pronounced increase in the company's summer condiment sales.

HUGE HOTEL GROUP—CUSTOMIZED CUSTOMER SERVICE

Who they are: Hotel and resorts properties managers.
What they do: They manager large hotel properties. Their customer services staffs range from 20 to 100.
What they wanted: To become more responsive to front desk customer problems, and to train customer service associates in proactive service and customer crisis management.

The Improv Focus
Two fundamental improv applications for customer service reside in hyperactive listening and responsive initiations. That is, improv artists hear the emotional context of individual initiations,

problems, and issues, align their responses for the most productive initiations, and then act on the input immediately. We
worked on question-and-answer games, expert-answer exercises,
and other responsive techniques to increase the comfort level and
speed of the associates' responses.

In business-improv teaching, we broke it down into steps and
then applied the games:

Step 1: Listen physically, using hyperactive listening techniques.

Step 2: Accept the emotional state of the customer/initiator.
Complement the emotional state of the customer through ownership and agreement. Resist the urge to close down or become
defensive. *Own this moment now!* This moment is *not like other moments;* this problem is *not the same as ones that occurred earlier.*
Even if the problem seems identical to past problems, improvisers must live in this moment. Every moment must live as its
own organic being; otherwise, we deprive ourselves of new experiences and lessons. If we do this—predict problems or assume solutions before they occur—we destroy the moments
and the experiences of our customers. We lose the partnership
and we lose their business.

Step 3: Act immediately on the issue. Every immediate step you
take toward the resolution of the issue is a visible, tangible sign
of your commitment to the customer/player relationship,
clearly demonstrating your desire to build a long-term partnership with the customer/player.

Step 4: Show them the steps you're taking—say them aloud.
Make promises you can keep and keep the promises you make.
Few customers anticipate full communication, so when they
receive it, you're not only building trust, you are also creating

an enormous distinction between you and your company as one entity and your competition as another.

Improv principles build empathy with the client/player, agreement and ownership of the problem, and immediate action toward resolutions.

IMPORTANT PHARMACEUTICAL COMPANY — PRESENTING TO A PROSPECT/SELLING ON CAMERA

Who they are:	Cutting-edge pharmaceutical salespeople.
What they do:	They sell pharmaceuticals by pitching new products to doctors via the company's live, interactive web site.
What they wanted:	To have the company's people become more at ease on camera. Also they wanted salespeople to become more spontaneous and relaxed in their videoconference sessions with doctor-customers through the very difficult medium of Internet webcast.
Some of the problems:	People delivering information through webcasts are boxed into a tiny square on the doctor's computer screen. The doctors are busy people with very little time. The doctors are also smart, important, successful, distracted, overworked, stressed, skeptical, a bit egotistical, and unvaryingly out of time.

137

The Improv Focus
In this program, we concentrated on presentation games that develop speed, quicker thinking, responsiveness, and flexibility. By appreciating the limited time opportunities with the doctors, we focused on getting to the point, dealing with immediate questions, and getting out before the stay was overdone.

PROFESSIONAL SPORTS ORGANIZATION—
PROGRAM RECOMMENDATIONS

Who they are:	A professional sports organization.
What they do:	They conduct rookie orientation programs.
What they wanted:	To highlight issues that rookie professional athletes face, as well as role-playing possible solutions to these issues.

The Improv Focus
Playing professional sports is a dream of many, but a reality for a very few. As we all know, sometimes the reality of a situation isn't exactly what we expected; this is certainly true in athletics. Many rookies are making the transition from teen to adulthood, from poverty to making a substantial income, sometimes with little or no mentoring in managing finances. Cultural and societal backgrounds vary widely among players and teams. There are pressures from friends and family because of their new-found success, from their on-the-field performance, and finally, from exposure to the media and the general responsibilities of being a celebrity.

138

We were able to use elements of humor and surprise to engage the audience, and broach otherwise-difficult subject matter with the rookies. As we've noted, comedy is uniquely disarming and our unique approach to creating realistic sketches portraying real-life situations allowed the scenes to resonate strongly with the audience in an entertaining and memorable forum.

Using improv, and suggestions from the audience that related to their issues, we were able to give real-time solutions that they could employ when faced with similar situations. This unique approach set the stage for deeper consultation with the advisors who were on site to coach the new players: psychiatrists, counselors, and experienced ex-players.

This workshop and the interactive games built awareness of the various problems, issues, and circumstances the new players will inevitably face in their professional and personal lives.

EXECUTIVE WOMEN'S SUMMIT

Who they are:	Chief-executive-level businesswomen.
What they do:	They manage a wide variety of diverse corporations and businesses.
What they wanted:	To develop greater communication skills that will aid in the management of their diverse staffs and lead to a more productive and creative work environment.

The Improv Focus

The benefits of learning improv for communication skills are immense. Effective improvisers are great listeners; applying improv techniques greatly increases the capacity to actively listen and respond. We concentrated on hyperactive listening—to not only hear the words that another player is offering, but to also understand the emotional context of what they mean. We worked exercises to teach flexibility in actions and responses in improv, in business, and in daily life.

CONSULTING GROUP AND THEIR CIO CLIENTS— BUILDING AND MANAGING CREATIVITY

Who they are: A really advanced business consulting firm and their CIO client base.

What they do: They provide strategic consulting in the technology field to more than 11,000 organizations worldwide.

What they wanted: To challenge client CIOs to better manage continuous organizational transformation for strategic success, and to help them learn new skills/techniques to attract the best talent to their organizations.

The Improv Focus

As we know, to make any scene, exercise, or game succeed the improviser must accept the other performers' initiations and then add his or her own ideas to them. If judgment, either external (what they are saying) or internal (what I am saying or am going to say), is present, then the scene/game will not be successful.

To help illustrate these principles, the CIOs worked through acceptance exercises: "One-Word Story," "Product-Selling Game," and movement games. With a tangible exercise illus-

140

trating the importance of accepting and then expressing their ideas without judgment, the CIOs were able to more easily incorporate change processes and provide practical insights/actionable tools for improved execution of organizational change initiatives.

PHARMACEUTICAL COMPANY—SALES/HOST TRAINING

Who they are: Global pharmaceutical company.

What they do: They are one of the world's fastest-growing pharmaceutical companies with a strong portfolio of products and a robust pipeline of new drugs in development.

What they wanted: Three goals were established for this training session.

1. To provide salespeople with specific steps they may take to initiate functional conversation with physicians attending association meetings and sociably educate them in the company's offerings (i.e., attract new customers).
2. To assist associates with selling/schmoozing/relationship techniques.
3. To create a platform of uniform, effective, repeatable sales steps for associates.

The Improv Focus

Our participants were immersed in exercises to help them to initiate, listen, and then act on what is said, instead of simply

141

waiting for the other person to stop and then adding what they wanted to say. Through the workshop, the associates came away with a better understanding of acting on their intuitive opportunities.

TOP AD AGENCY—
ROLE PLAY REAL WORLD

Who they are: One of the top-three ad agencies.

What they do: They trade teams from the agency's creative and sales departments.

What they wanted: To pump up their traditional staff training by implementing a range of improv offerings.

The Improv Focus

In this case, we used brainstorming, presentation, and improv role-play techniques that allowed creative and sales-pitch teams to bring actual, current presentation problems for work-shopping. We also added basic presentation games to increase comfort. This is where we were able to put the "show" back in their business.

CONCLUSION

These are just a few examples of the virtually limitless applications of improv that help make organizations more nimble, flexible, spontaneous, and creative. Perhaps the most important aspect of organizations embracing improv as part of the culture is that they can incorporate improv as a tool *before* it is needed.

By learning and applying improv basics, these organizations can then employ it when and where improv is most valuable: during times of change, stress, and crisis. They've learned the lessons they'll need to adapt to change. They increase their improvability and are better able to handle transformation as a business practice.

More Improvercises

Well, you did a good job working through your first improv lesson in Chapter 6. In this chapter, you'll find a range of additional exercises that will stretch you in new, different, and possibly weirder ways. These exercises are based on the fundamentals from your earlier lessons and will assist with even more business applications. As always, it helps to work through these challenges with your emerging improv-ensemble.

MORE EXERCISES

Games are endless in form and function. The games and exercises we employ as ensemble toolsets permit players to interact in unique, creative experiences. These exercises also increase skill in specific areas of improvability. Mostly though, games are meant to be played with frequency and consistency to build deeper connections of trust, communication, and resourceful releases among players as a group and as individuals. The ensemble can always be sharpened; these games are the grindstone.

Here's a brief list of purposes for the following improv exercises:

- Introduce new concepts, forms, and options to players.
- Build more skills through a variety of principle applications.
- Sharpen team abilities through repetition and practice.

Frequent practice and application, at the most basic levels, will assist with every level of improvisation, especially in the areas of agreement and acceptance. In the beginning of our improv studies, it's hard to consistently agree to agree; it's hard to always say *yes* to any initiation. Our judgment system jumps in to bite us right in our creativity. We suddenly think:

"This won't work."

"That can't happen."

"I've never seen that before."

"What does that even mean?"

Moments of improvisation are unique—the substance and circumstances can't be recreated. By initiating (developing your own creations) while accepting (listening to, processing, and incorporating) someone else's initiations, you are now practicing the basis of group improvisation. Through consistent application and patient repetition of improv principles, we build the speed and strength of our improv reflexes. Let the games begin (again).

146

NEW OBJECT NAME AND APPLICATION

- *Theory.* One function of improv is synthesis; other purposes include mutation, evolution, and comedy. This game falls into the mutation category—changing an element to something new.
- *Objective.* The process is twofold: to accept stuff that already exists but to recreate it for some weird and wonderful end result.
- *Action.* Play this game with the same format as the product-selling game in Chapter 6 (see page 102). Recall that we created a product that couldn't be sold. In this game we create a new name and application for an item that already exists. Agree on one product: snow, cheese, charcoal—any functional and well-known item. Using group brainstorm and improv techniques, generate a new name, function, and identity for the new product.
- *Coaching.* As with all group brainstorming, allow many ideas to exist at first, then whittle them down to a manageable amount. Encourage play within the group. The best results you can hear are laughter and excitement from a small group at work.

IMAGINARY AD GAME

- *Theory.* We want to provide freedom from every perceived limitation, physical and otherwise. Imagination begins by envisioning what can be.
- *Objective.* First, this is fun. Second, it frees the group from physical limitations of actual items.
- *Action.* Play this game as a variation of the product-selling game. But in this particular game, instead of coming up with

a product that can't be sold, evolve an ad campaign with no product or service whatsoever. Provide all the benefits, qualities, slogans, ads, and more with no end product, only the benefits and reasons to buy.

- *Coaching.* Encourage the players of this game to amplify the benefits and traits of the product beyond any logic or reasoning. We're specifically trying to explore what isn't, instead of what is.

BAD AD PRODUCT GAME

- *Theory.* By turning something over, by revolving an object to view its other odd, weird sides, we see more of the object's facets. We discover more about it and can add more to it.
- *Objective.* Upend the normally accepted, positive benefits and applications of products and create one that is awful and does bad things.
- *Action.* Play this as a variation of the product-selling game, but in this adaptation create a negative product and ad campaign. In other words, generate a product that does everything wrong, bad, terrible, or worse.
- *Coaching.* Stretch conceptions; keep it light and fun.

OPPOSITE SIDE SPEECH

- *Theory.* Moving away from personal convictions exposes us to new directions and stimuli.
- *Objective.* Force the opposite side to succeed.
- *Action.* In this game, each player chooses the opposite side of what we would normally consider a nonissue (e.g., freedom is a good thing; life is too short; pets are good companions)

and presents a defense with full commitment. ("In reality, freedom is dangerous because. . . .")

- *Coaching.* Allow the audience to have fun but keep the presenters "in character." The speakers must stick to their side of the issue, despite its obvious wrongheadedness. They succeed when they're convincing in their delivery and position.

ARGUMENTS

- *Theory.* We build nimble and committed agreement by accepting input from everyone and everything, suspending our conscious value systems to access our intuition.
- *Objective.* The side players will engage the center player in a discussion, trying to convince the center player of their position. The center player should keep both conversations going at the same time and attempt to agree with both positions simultaneously.
- *Action.* Three players—one in the center, two on either side. The side players will take two opposite sides of the same argument—gun control, yes/no; legalize marijuana, yes/no; or similar debate positions.
- *Coaching.* This is an almost impossible situation for the center player, but that's the idea. Encourage the center player to keep logical and emotional agreement with both side players. It will take a lot of concentration and focus. That's part of the fun.

MOVING THROUGH—STREAM OF CONSCIOUSNESS 1

- *Theory.* Random offerings gravitate toward each other. We want to rebalance people and groups as much as possible; avoid logic by introducing chaos.

149

- *Objective.* The idea is to achieve a communal stream of consciousness from the offerings and movement of the group.
- *Action.* Groups of four or more will move in nonlinear directions around the working space. As players move, they should seek a communal tempo to the action—players moving at the same speed but not in the same directions. Players move past each other and through the space in random directions. As players move, they will offer words or thoughts out loud based on a central theme or image: red, food, light, chill, or go, for example.
- *Coaching.* Players may feed off the initiations of others, but it's also important to encourage fractured and disparate input from each person. The idea is to seek radical incursions into normal thoughts.

MOVING THROUGH—STREAM OF CONSCIOUSNESS 2

- *Theory.* Revolutionary concepts arrive from unusual activities.
- *Objective.* Similar to the first version, we're trying to fragment thoughts into emotional images and less-structured offerings.
- *Action.* Virtually the same as the previous game, except that in this case the players will freeze when individual players offer a word or sound to the group. The game action should resume—each player starting a new movement—as soon as the new sound is heard and incorporated into the activity.
- *Coaching.* It may be helpful to alternate the speed of this game: fast, slow, slower, and so on, as the game is in progress. This will advance the fragmented quality of the output while keeping the group off balance.

150

LIFTING A PLAYER

- *Theory.* Trust is fundamental to ensemble creation and maintenance. Players will risk more of themselves and each other when trust is a fundamental component of their interaction.
- *Objective.* This is a basic trust exercise. The idea is to get players to interact through odd and unusual ways.
- *Action.* Groups of five or more will lift one player off his feet. The volunteer should go limp, allowing the group to move him. The group will turn the player over, feet over head or vice versa, then set him back on his feet.
- *Coaching.* Move the volunteer in different directions. Keep him safe and secure, but vary the direction, distance, and ways that you move him.

TWO PLAYERS — ONE VOICE

- *Theory.* Give-and-take is an integral element to every creative process. We get caught up in our own voices so often and so easily that sometimes we lose track of the rest of the world. This game forces us to share our voice and ideas.
- *Objective.* The idea is to create one voice, one idea, one story from two different players. Each must offer and accept at the same time, while studying the other player for direction, intention, and input.
- *Action.* Two players face each other, establishing eye contact. They begin a series of sentences based on a central topic: "Nice day today," "What a wonderful lunch," or "I had this great idea," for example. The players create and offer the same words at the same time, evolving the words into sentences and then stories.

151

- *Coaching.* Players will think this game impossible the first time they try it—it's pretty tough to get two people to speak coordinately. But the game is anything but impossible. It takes concentration, giving, and taking all at the same time.

CONCLUSION

Trust doesn't happen by accident. In order to trust, players must feel a compelling sense of security with their partners. In order to ask someone to trust you, you must provide that person with the security to do so. This is *your* responsibility, not theirs.

In ensemble work, trust is an active, organic component. People must know they can risk—and be supported in their risks. If they aren't supported, or don't feel they're supported, they will not risk—and perhaps they shouldn't.

CHAPTER 11

Managing the Emperors

Players, you have my permission to become more inventive, creative, and imaginative. The imaginative part is going to be the hardest one because it's the most difficult to quantify and it's also the one for which businesses have the least patience.

Typical managers want their people to be imaginative—to use their creative intuition—but logic, order, and authority are the very elements that defy and oppose imagination. It's the rare company that provides time to muse or be amused. Still, in order to access and improve our improv skills, we need to build time for just these things.

The work begins at the ground floor. Don't wait for management to come to you with the imagination programs. If you do, you'll be waiting for a long time.

In every facet of your creative life, the responsibility begins with you. You must initiate, you must offer, you must begin to build the infrastructure of play. You may *not* wait for your environment to change; you must change it yourself (without alienating anyone—remember, the people you meet on your way up the ladder of success are usually the same ones you meet on the way down if you fall, just as you need their help). This can and will be done with good taste, perseverance, and a sense of humor.

Yet we all allow ourselves reasons and excuses why we don't change the environment from one of anxious repetition to one of unusual creation. We all have the same arguments and conditions:

- I am not working in a creative environment.
- Everyone here says they want new ideas, but they really don't.
- There's always a reason not to do something new.
- I don't have authority or seniority to change things.
- I'm too new or not new enough or the porridge is too cold . . .

In reality, these are nonarguments, excuses in support of the status quo. In my seminars, questions and comments about how to break the cycle of lethargy abound:

- "What do you do with a boss who won't even let you finish describing the idea before he kills it?"
- "Is there any way to handle a manager who doesn't tell you what's wrong with the proposal? She just wants to see others."
- "Our directors say they want us to think outside the box but whenever we show them anything different, they hate it."
- "The vice-president ridicules anything new or creative."
- "Do you have any doughnuts?"

I can't help with the last question, but the rest of them I've got covered. Typical management structures require managers to *stay out* of specific creative processes—creative development is handled by teams who report development to managers. While apparently efficient, this separation of authority and responsibility promotes a subtly antagonistic relationship between Creators/Players and the Judges/Roman Emperors: "You do the ideas. I'll judge them."

The consequences of this Roman Emperor syndrome form the basis for disillusionment in creative processes and are a leading cause of talent drain in creative organizations. We must remanage this system in order to allow innovation to exist and flourish.

TECHNIQUES TO MANAGE THE ROMAN EMPERORS

Here's the dilemma: managers who are responsible for managing creative processes, yet aren't actively invested in specific processes, thereby creating our Roman Emperor syndrome. You're cornered into producing something new for people who may or may not truly want new or even anything like new.

But a manager who invests time, even strictly observation time, with a group creative process will be dramatically more disposed to accepting the results than one who doesn't. Managers who invest time in the creative process not only observe the end results but also see the effort necessary to achieve innovation. They build a visceral connection to the work and a bond with the people generating it.

It's vital for managers to observe the execution and effort of the creative processes of their groups. Some systems directly oppose this idea; they assert that managers will make more in-formed decisions by remaining separate from the generation process, thereby achieving greater objectivity toward the ulti-mate judgments. This notion is just plain wrong and sometimes just plain dumb.

Theatrical directors must see the show in previews, work with the cast in rehearsals, and revise the script in read-throughs. They must involve themselves in every facet of the production creative process or they've forgone their artistic re-sponsibilities. Again, this doesn't suggest that the director must *do the work* in each area (designers design, writers write), but directors have to understand the process in order to synthesize and support it.

Here are some basics in managing a creative process. By ap-plying these techniques, the likelihood of the Emperor accepting your output will increase dramatically:

1. *Invite the Emperors in, involving them directly in the creative process.* If your creative process time allotment is an hour, request that the Emperors spend 15 minutes listening and observing, offering ideas and input. Like everyone else, they may not judge ideas during this process. They're there for added input and observation only. As you've done for the rest of the group, share the rules of the creative process with the Emperors: no judging, add to ideas, support initia-tions, accept ideas, initiate, and explore.

2. *Lure Emperors away from the darkness, into the light.* It's a law of business nature that most managers *want* to be part of the process but most of them don't know how—it embarrasses them. You must *lead them* as you want to be led. Here's some dialogue that may help:

156

We know how important this creative process is. We could really use your ideas and input for a few minutes during our brainstorming session. You don't have to stay the entire time; in fact, we'll be moving pretty quickly onto other areas. But your investment in the process will show everyone our priorities and I think you'll see some great stuff, too.

3. *Establish objective criteria.* It's critical that the objectives of the creative process be established and shared with the entire group. You want the team to know, specifically, when it has achieved the desired results. The criteria should be objective—goals posted clearly and explicitly—and ones on which everyone agrees. We're trying to delay subjective judgment as long as possible (I like/don't like it). Assessment of results is usually a combination of the two (I think it works and I like it). But it's critical that objectivity and subjectivity be balanced during the creative process. This ensures that players understand, logically and emotionally, the process and goals of creativity.

WHAT HAPPENS WHEN THIS HAPPENS

The client or boss or customer or manager says, "We need new thinking, new ideas. I'm tired of the same old, same old. Let's get out of this rut. I want you people to [everyone inhale deeply] think outside the box."

You take this direction on faith—the boss wants you to come up with radically new ideas. And you do. And you present them. And virtually everyone in the room is aghast at the new ideas: "Too radical. . . . Not our style. . . . Departure from our past. . . . What the hell is that?"

We return to our business paradox:

- To be identified by our audience, we must be distinctive.
- In order to become distinctive, we must innovate.
- Innovation by definition demands that we move away from what we're used to.
- What we're used to got us here in the first place.
- In order to get to the next place, we have to innovate.
- We want to innovate but not so much that we aren't who we were.
- Yesterday doesn't mean anything—at least in comparison to tomorrow.

In this case, "management" as a concept (not necessarily managers as individuals) is in the way. At times like this, the most important thing a manager can do (the manager in this case is the personification of "management") to support the creative process is to get the heck out of the way—become an nonimpediment. The flow of improv information generates its own energy. Once the energy is building, the work moves in many directions at the same time. The human/managerial temptation is to steer the energy toward what is perceived to be a useful direction. While this temptation is understandable, it must be resisted.

As has been noted elsewhere, all innovation is either initiating or accepting. You are either coming up with the idea or heightening the offerings of your fellow players. This is the basis for truly useful innovative activity; this is the very heart of improvisation. Management, by definition, includes many other priorities and motives. When improvising, you must literally go with the flow.

ALTERNATING RESPONSIBILITY

Improv action sessions have a beginning, middle, and end. The great majority of applications—idea generation, team building, communication, and strategizing—can be accomplished within specific time frames. (It's worth noting, however, that sessions without specific time limitations can be a dynamic device for envelope stretching and snow-globe shaking.) The logistical needs, agenda, schedule, and related responsibilities should be rotated among the team players. By alternating responsibilities, players develop deeper investment and appreciation in the overall mission of the group. As important, rotating responsibilities circumvents the stagnation that can occur with repetitive or mundane roles. As manager, allow the group to establish its own momentum within the context of the mission.

Teaching yourself to get the heck out of the way can be a frustrating, even maddening, experience. Managers are taught, even paid, to manage, and manage they will, sometimes to the detriment of innovation and improvisation. In order to fulfill this manifest destiny, we feel that if we aren't managing, we aren't discharging our responsibilities, or performing our duties. There's also a powerful emotional drive in the execution of management. It's satisfying, sometimes exciting and even rewarding when the job is well done and you've been a contributing director. We are control freaks because we like to control freaks. And we're darned good at it. We want to get in the driver's seat because we like to drive.

CONCLUSION

The world needs managers. After all, somebody's got to tell everyone else when the job is done. Good managers direct peo-

159

ple, nurture positive input, affirm good decisions, provide permission to accomplish, establish the need to risk, and balance roles, responsibilities, and efforts. Good managers are like good parents: They create us and set the rules. They help us when we need it, nudge us when we falter, and, most important, tell us when we've done well. The talent of a great manager lies in timing: when to direct and when to let go.

CHAPTER 12

The Case for Comedy

HUMOR AS A LIFESTYLE

While this book is not intended as a psycho/sociological treatise, when dealing with behavioral changes we inevitably bump against parallel disciplines and theories. As you've already seen, I borrow liberally from other areas of study to suit my own nefarious or hilarious purposes. While there is a wide source of materials available on the subject of humor—and even more devoted to comedy—these sources generate their conclusions empirically. Scientists analyze humor from the outside in—they view the activity of humor and study its cause and effect on subjects.

With all the humility I can muster (painfully little), I study humor, comedy, and improvisation as a *practitioner*: technician, advocate, teacher, and monk. Literally from childhood, I made the conscious decision to embrace humor as a way of life, to study and apply it as my vocation. (I also promised to use the power of humor only for good, in the best interests of all humankind.)

The vast majority of theory, however, misses the fundamental necessity of humor in human culture, its imperative, elemental presence in our world. Even in the smallest incident of everyday life, humor's presence is recognized, desired, and rewarded. The absence of humor is an indelible signal of negativity: stress, pressure, discomfort, fear, and worse.

Humor is a universal and fundamentally necessary component of human life. It is a common trait found in virtually every culture and society in the world. As natural as breathing, the bizarre physical expression of laughter presents itself in every language, religion, race, nationality, and continent of the world. The simple act of smiling is one of the first activities humans grasp; cognition begins through humor; humor equals happiness. The cyclical desire for humor goes on and on. (If only we would continue this practice throughout our education, business, and lives.)

The fundamental necessity of humor remains strikingly consistent through time and trials. While the subjects and applications of humor vary widely from culture to culture, the functions of humor are strikingly similar. In the collective human psyche, humor serves several vital functions:

- *Coping mechanism.* Humor allows us to manage, accept, or tolerate subjects that we wouldn't or couldn't accept in any other way: death, war, tragedy, loss. Subjects that are too preposterously large and forbidding for normal comprehension, issues too gruesome to contemplate with any reasonable perspective—these issues are often reduced to manageable concepts through humor. One ancient comedy rule goes: Tragedy plus time equals comedy.

- *Diminishment of stress, fear, and danger.* Laughing in the dark, giggling at a funeral, chuckling after a brush with death, are all manifestations of humor's power to assist us in managing our minds.
- *Healing.* Laughter, in addition to recharging our physiology, promotes personal well-being in individuals. As important, environments that promote a sense of humor are more productive, efficient, healthy, and profitable.
- *Catharsis.* Humor provides release of tension, stress, and pressure from a wide variety of difficult stimuli.
- *Diversion.* Humor allows us to take time off from the demands of the world around us.
- *Acceptance.* Humor allows us to understand the frailty and faults in our humanity and in ourselves: greed, lust, duplicity, and so on.

THE DYNAMICS OF LAUGHTER

A group of strangers is acting through a common reflex. First there is the humorous occurrence—the joke or incident. There is a brief moment of comprehension, acceptance of the act and subject. The reference is registered and accepted. Surprise occurs. (Comedy is built on the foundation of unusual associations—humans and businesspeople alike are attracted to surprise. Unusual associations provide stimulation and delight for the recipients. The resolution of these associations is a device for the generation of comedy. Unusual associations are also a source for innovation and idea generation.) Then there is the human reflex of laughter: Individually, the head moves back and up; the mouth opens for quick and sharp inhalation; and the lungs and diaphragm expand quickly. Then the physical expression occurs: Mouth is open, smile rises, eyes squint; breath is expelled rapidly with the universal staccato laughter sounds; the head moves forward; the torso contracts as the laughter continues.

Identifying recognition occurs; shared and sharing moments of community are born. In the communal interaction of comedy, we typically desire understanding, acceptance, and/or recognition from others surrounding us. We either want everyone to know that we "got the joke" or we want to help them "get the joke." We want to communicate the reference that is the crux of the comedy moment or we want it communicated to us. This is very powerful, intimate interacting; it is reference-building and educational for the audience. But it is also much more personal—a very intimate sharing of intellect, many times among total strangers. It is difficult to overestimate the importance and value of this interaction.

The very physiology of laughter has profound effects on people. Laughter opens and powers the lungs, stimulates heart and organs. It wakes and shakes people up in a positive and incredibly beneficial way.

HUMOR ATTRACTS

As we've discussed, humor is a necessary facet of a business personality. If your business is too buttoned-down, it's harder to attract talented people, new customers, and radical ideas. On the other hand, a business with a functional sense of humor provides balance, releases anxieties and tension, and acts more nimbly through distress. If your business lacks a sense of humor, go out and get one—it will invariably increase your communication, innovation, and human resource capital.

HUMOR VERSUS COMEDY

In our quest to improvise well, it's important to create a distinction between a sense of humor — the ability and desire to perceive something with wit, play, or exuberant amusement — and comedy — a specific mechanical device in the humor toolbox.

BRIEF DIGRESSION

The public perception of modern comedy is not very high, with good reason. In recent generations, the comedy industry has catered to the dumbest, lowest-denominator content. Comedy, as an industry, has created the perception that in order to be funny, you must ridicule someone, place dumb people in idiotic situations, or suspend common sense to the point of painful absurdity.

Stupidity is a very small niche of the total comic spectrum. There are many subjects to investigate and elevate through a sensible application of humor, and limitless sources of comedy material in the world around us, *especially in the business world:* ever-tightening deadlines and budgets, incessant travel, communication devices that don't communicate, computers, commuting, training, meetings, continuing education, to name just a few. By focusing on the comedic conditions of our lives and employing an intelligent perspective toward the material, we can generate comedy that's not only useful, but illuminating as well.

Comedy should be a noble pursuit—it's too important to treat cavalierly. It has the capacity to make the world not only more tolerable, but positively enjoyable. We must employ comedy responsibly, with good taste and a mostly dignified approach. It doesn't have to offend people; in fact, we should choose not to offend when possible. (On the other hand, comedy should offend people that need offending.)

Comic—arousing or deserving of laughter.
—Webster's Dictionary

Comedy examines subjects for the purpose of challenging commonly held assumptions. It tilts the perspective of its target to show unexpected facets and implications of the subject or situation. Comedy's job is to get us to look at common things in a different way. Comedy shows you something you already know in a way that you never saw it before. When this occurs, you experience surprise, recognition, and a "Ha! I've never thought of it that way" moment. Through this small illumination, comedy leads us to comprehension and understanding. At its best, comedy opens our eyes and if we're lucky it sometimes can correct our vision, too.

CULTIVATING A CORPORATE SENSE OF HUMOR

A *sense of humor* is the ability to perceive the people, situations, and world around you with wit—the ability to amuse and perceive what is amusing. To *amuse* is to engage or occupy in an agreeable way.

Humor is also an access mechanism, providing people with a path to experience new stimuli, challenges, and sensations. It provides a bond that links people together through empathy and understanding. You've heard the advice that it's best to start a speech with a joke; the very purpose of this device is to create an agreeable bond with the audience, to engage them in an agreeable way.

A sense of humor is inclusive—it brings people together. It's attractive; people like people with a sense of humor. Consider the power of humor. When executed correctly, it can unite hundreds, even thousands of people in a common action: laughter. A sense of humor is compelling. It holds attention. It's an essential tool, offering a comical perspective on subjects that would otherwise frustrate or enrage people.

A sense of humor is healing. If you need proof, rent any of the Robin Williams movies where he plays the quirky doctor who restores health through humor. All kidding aside, humor benefits health, builds a positive environment, and nurtures rewarding relationships.

Most important, people with a sense of humor are intellectual, active, and fast. They are quick to think and quicker to act. They manage negatives better and communicate more easily. They're freer and they free people around them.

A PLEA FOR HUMOR

The business world desperately needs more humor. Entire industries and career disciplines, even economic sectors are completely devoid of a sense of humor. Take architecture, for example. Billions of dollars are spent each year in the design of new buildings. The science and art of architecture requests that buildings should be designed for safety, functionality, and appeal. While many buildings may be aesthetically appealing, very few are designed with a sense of wit, whimsy, or humor. I'm personally planning to turn the antennae at the top of the John Hancock Building into football goal posts, complete with ball sailing through the uprights.

This isn't to say that architects themselves have no sense of humor; many are hilarious, talented people. And I know they come up with amusing designs. We have to convince the developers that we need a bit of wit.

Humor Values

Anyone in retail sales, branding, and marketing will tell you that the consumer's attention span, already hummingbird-like, continues to shrink in rapidly diminishing cycles. Competition is ever greater for an audience's attention and it's nearly impossible to cut through the clutter. In this amusement economy, it's our responsibility to capture and hold the audience's attention—even if the awareness duration is painfully short. Humor captures people's attention. A sense of humor attracts and holds them.

Humor is the most underutilized human emotion. Every day we're exposed to a wide range of stresses: frustration, tension, grief, anger, and more. We view these conditions as a natural component of life, accepting them as the normal state of the real world. We, especially in business, need to combat anxiety with the tools available: humor, play, and fun. We're pretty good at adding stress to the world around us; we need to get better at contributing delight.

One of our missions in this book is to use the torch of humor to light a path of innovation and comical inspiration for the business world. We can kill drudgery, staleness, even despair by having more fun with ourselves and each other.

Acquire the Sense

It's essential to understand that it's actually possible to *build a sense of humor*. Regardless of your perception, a sense of humor isn't something you have or you don't have. If you don't have it, you can get it. We see this all the time in the comedy world—a painfully shy and retiring person who, through the experiences of improv and theater, blossoms into a brilliant comedy performer. Many performers are personally reclusive until they free themselves through a performance sense of humor. It's a basic form of expression and therapy for comics and actors.

Your business has a personality. Your division, your team, your group has its own distinct character. The components of this group personality can be refined, heightened, educated, directed, and shaped. Just as you can change yourself for the better, you can inspire your group as well. You can build a personal sense of humor and you can inject a sense of humor into the world around you. It is especially easy to produce and promote a sense of humor in your group and the business world in general precisely because there is so little of it in business today. It's easy to fill the voids because, in business, there are so many of them.

Consider the people you know with a good sense of humor. They're quick-witted, spontaneous, active, intellectual, funny, and direct. We're drawn to people like that and if we're lucky, they become our friends and our partners. People with a good sense of humor are sensitive. They have a brain and wit, but they also have great ears. *They listen to you.* It's simply easier to employ humor from someone else's content, so people with a good sense of humor listen and apply the humor as easily to your subjects as to theirs. This trait creates a special bond between people. It's one way we become friends.

Does your team listen to itself and the outside world? Is your group attentive and open? Is your team quick-witted, spontaneous, funny, and direct? Some of the individuals may be, but regarding the general personality of the group, does it operate in activity, with a sense of humor, right here and right now? Does it freely debate, does it risk, does it push and pull its members with a sense of fun? It should do these things on purpose—not by accident.

FUN HELPS

Enjoyment helps a sense of humor. Having fun with the subject matter helps people access it. Conversely, a dry subject delivered with serious gravity bores the heck out of normal people. Your first responsibility, when building a business sense of humor, is to consider the delivery of your subject matter using fun devices: Convene the meeting on the floor; bring hot dogs for everyone's lunch; start the brainstorm session on the roof. As Marshall McLuhan said, the medium is the message, so how you deliver it is as important as what you deliver. Your job, should you choose to accept it, is to raise the stakes of your delivery mechanisms.

Southwest Airlines understands the power of a sense of humor. Because it translates the "seat-belt" speech into an entertaining and humorous moment, it actually *gets people to pay attention to a message that they've all heard a jillion times!* It amuses, it holds your attention through a functional use of humor. Imagine the possibilities if you could hold the attention of your customers, associates, audience, and/or subordinates in the same way. What if you had the power and talent to capture and keep their interest? If you have a sense of humor you'll be more successful.

LOSE THE FEAR

Improvisation should be fun and exciting. It's supposed to be a bit scary. For some people, it's nearly impossible to improvise because of their fear of vulnerability. But fear is not a sufficient reason to avoid improv. It's important for us to face our fears. Through these challenges we grow. We must enjoy improv. We all have a responsibility to make it fun for ourselves and our associates.

We all have the responsibility to make our jobs and work environments more fun, or at the very least, less miserable than they sometimes become. The conditions of fun, enjoyment, amusement, and humor are too serious to take lightly or ignore. If you've walked out of a job from hell or if you've watched huge turnover at a company, odds are there was no fun involved in the job. The skeptics are now yelling, "Hey! Work is work; fun is fun. Who says they're supposed to meet?" Well *I* say so, that's who. If you want to attract good people, new customers, better ideas, a new market, a new demo- or psychographic, you have to attract them with some fun, play, wit, or humor. If you build the playground, they will come.

When you were in school, there were a few teachers who *really* got the lessons across; they were the ones with passion, with fire, and maybe most important, they were the ones who had fun with the subjects. You connected with their sense of fun and it made the material much easier to digest.

One result of comedy is laughter. Laughter forms community in an audience: a tangible visceral shared experience that becomes a frame of reference and memory for what was once a group of strangers. People bond through laughter. My business is the generation and execution of comic materials for audience consumption. If we've done something elevating and useful and the audience participates in laughter, we've done well. One of our primary objectives is to engage the audience through laughter and shared experience. This is my function in life.

ARE WE HAVING FUN YET?

A primary benefit of studying improvisation in groups is that the group gets to laugh together. The benefits of this interaction are too many to list, but they're real and powerful. Typical responses to our live workshops are phrases like: "I've never had so much fun. . . . I didn't know we could actually *enjoy* being with each other. . . . I've always known we could have a good time together; we just never have before. . . ."

Managers, consider this point for a moment! Do your people ever have fun together? on purpose? Do you plan for play, fun, humor, laughter, or maybe just some happiness? The business world certainly demands a lot of everything else: heightened stress, increasing production, greater commitment, on and on and on. Do you plan for even the slightest iota of fun or funny?

The more fun, exciting, and rewarding the creative process is, the better the end results. This is not rocket science, just some simply uncommon sense.

STEPS TO ALLOW YOUR BUSINESS TO IMPROVISE

In order to lay the blueprint and groundwork for improvising in business, here are some basic rules:

- *Improvisation and innovation do not recognize hierarchy or authority.* In years past, when decision making was centralized, decisions and doctrine passed down from the top. This system works if you have the one brain at the top that is smarter, faster, nimbler than the rest of your organization. Today, we employ the collective brain of the organization for wider reference and more power. Improv recognizes stimuli from every direction, so expertise, and more important, authority are irrelevant to the process. Initiations can and must come from everywhere and everyone. This poses myriad delicate political issues: Managers want to retain their status; experts want to retain their expertise. For an organization to improvise, though, everyone must contribute to the center of the circle. Individuals immerse their own egos in the larger activity. This builds trust, security in the group, and more risk-taking within the organization.

- *Everyone must play.* If you've got a boss who wants everyone to get with the teamwork program but can't take the time himself, well, you've got a problem. The same is true with improvisation. Drag the boss in, preferably kicking and screaming. He doesn't have to stay or even have to like it, but he has to invest some time in it. More important, if you've got 30 people in a room, *all of them must improvise.* You can't allow 4 people to "just watch" while 26 people work. Improv is ensemble work; everyone pulls at the oars equally. People are reluctant to play in improv because they're holding onto their internal perceptions, worried they'll seem foolish. We've already established that value judgments have to go out the window, so get everyone playing. You'll find some gems in the reluctant ones and the results will be greater throughout the organization. Remember, we're talking productivity here. We can all immerse our egos in that subject.
- *Consistency helps.* Schedule time for people to play, muse, consider, and brainstorm *when they don't need to!* As managers, we typically ask people to become innovative after desperation sets in. For best spontaneity and improv results, hone the skills of your players *before* you ask them for miracles.

CONCLUSION

Encourage play; start fun. Cultivate a sense of humor in yourself and those around you. By applying these concepts, your environment begins to encourage innovation, you build smarter people, and you will have more fun yourself. It works.

CHAPTER 13

Improvisation in Presentations

As we've discovered, the definition of improvisation is to invent, compose, or recite without preparation. The function of a business presentation is to communicate messages without putting the audience to sleep. Building a connection with an audience usually assumes and requires a great deal of preparation. In fact, it is virtually impossible for a typical business person to overrehearse a presentation. It is possible, if not likely, for people to rehearse *poorly*, but overrehearsing is rarely an issue. In order to apply improv to presentations, we practice games and exercises that free our choices of delivery, responding, and adaptation. We employ improv as an operating mechanism for our presentations.

Ideally, in order to have greatest impact, we hope to engage our audience on both a logical and emotional basis. The logical aspects of our presentation offer the reasons why people should become engaged. The emotional underpinnings are how and why people change their behavior. Remember, people choose to do something based on their *emotions* more than they choose things based on logic.

To successfully apply improvisation in business, we face interesting challenges: Since improvisation is invention without preparation, then we must rehearse being unprepared. We place ourselves in improv situations in which we have no clear direction, no prepared roadmap. We trust our intuition, brains, and training, relying on our guts and reflexes as much as our prepared materials. We're immersed in the age of "short-attention-span" audiences. You've got about 30 seconds to grab their interest and then you've got to keep it.

DISCOVERING DIRECTION

As we explore improv as a presentation tool, we agree on the context: It is the art of spontaneous creation within the context of a form or framework. This agreement to improvise naturally leads us to embrace a functional sense of humor: the choice to consider a subject, circumstance, or issue in a creative or comical manner, an active choice to "lighten up." Humor and improv are inextricably linked—the well-timed quip, retort, or observation is a prized technique in any live-communication setting. Moreover, improv also serves to loosen the audience, reducing tension and anxiety by creating a less formal, more relaxed atmosphere.

Finally, great presenters become great improvisers—one leads to the other as organic components of the same process. In acting, being in the moment allows even the actor to explore the character she is portraying. The art of acting means that the character is discovering moments *with the audience!* Great presenters embrace the same abilities—they *want* to enjoy the moment; they *need* to create an organic, sincere time in space; they *love* the excitement of the event. Pursuit of improv training builds this in every student.

Here are five applications for improv in presentations.

1. Improvisation is used to create a more relaxed, less strict atmosphere. By shedding the restrictions of a word-for-word script, speakers create a less formal, more accessible atmosphere. Accomplished presenters employ wide-ranging bullet points or general notes in their speeches and deliveries, as opposed to word-for-word text, to promote a more informal and more personal tone of delivery. Repetition of improv exercises builds confidence for speakers to employ these tactics and directions.

2. Improvisation comes to the rescue when the unexpected occurs: technical problems, questions, interruptions. Experienced improvisers are better able to confidently handle disruptions, distractions, and meltdowns. They are practiced "in the moment" so they are also able to adapt to new moments as they occur.

3. Improv sharpens the ability to respond to questions, comments, and changing circumstances. The practice of improv is the acceptance of constant change, so improvisers include change as part of their repertoire.

4. Improvisation creates dramatic opportunities. Like any other dramatic or comic device, improv is used to intentionally highlight moments of our choosing.

5. Improv indicates comprehension, intellectual ability, and much more. We prize improvability in our leaders: "She's so good thinking on her feet . . ."; "He's never at a loss for

words or action. . . ." The presenter who is responsive and adaptive to changing circumstances, the presenter who works the moment, instead of letting it work him, these are the prized players in our world.

Regarding item 1, it is important to rehearse as if the speech were entirely scripted. In practice and rehearsal sessions, fully visualize the audience and your relationship to them. Since the tone will be informal, move away from the podium or use it from the side. Allow for more movement and more contact with the audience. But be aware of too much movement. Improvisers are aware of the precise movements they need to communicate their intentions. They practice physical techniques that become the basis for their scenes. In your presentations, use direct, conscious motions to underscore your points. Eliminate any *unnecessary* motion.

STICK TO THE POINTS

Though an improv tone is less formal, have your bullet points clearly scripted and timed for yourself. Use images — a storyboard — next to the points to make certain you stay on track. Time your points, as well, for the same reason — to stay on track. As with all presentations, it's helpful to list an agenda of points for your audience as well.

In every presentation, use as few words as possible to make your point. Many people assume that restating a point adds emphasis — this is rarely the case. Imagine "Alas poor Yorick, I knew him well . . . really well . . . really, really well . . . we were very close . . . I knew him when we were kids. . . ." You get my drift.

Regarding item 2 on our list, using improvisation to manage interruptions or unexpected issues, there are several brief tips:

- Understand the problem — what is happening. Get your information quickly and clearly.
- Explain the situation to the audience as clearly as possible.
- Explain what the resolution or action will be.
- Do not repeat yourself more than once!
- Move to other topics as necessary.
- If all else fails, give your audience a break until the situation is resolved.

In order to be in the moment you need to know what that moment is. Get the information as soon as you can, relay it, and deal with it. If you *must* apologize to the audience, do it once and leave it alone.

If possible, continue with the presentation or relevant information. For example, if your PowerPoint display fails, move to another portion of the presentation that is less dependent on the technology and go back later to pick up the earlier points. It's even better to continue as you were, without the visual displays. This will take more work from your side (remember to rehearse interruptions), but the audience will appreciate your ongoing efforts.

In theater, if the scenery snaps in half, the crew will simply close the curtain and the cast will continue dialogue and action in front of it. In dire situations, a stage manager or principal actor will take the stage, explaining the situation to the audience, and move on with the work. If all your options fail, allow the audience to take a break or talk among themselves until the situation is resolved.

MORE CASES FOR COMEDY

Presenters incorporate comedy into their presentations for many useful reasons: Comedy is universal, catalyzing, and energizing. Well-crafted comedy is one of the most powerful mechanisms for delivering messages known to humankind. Having said that, comedy also contains inherent risks; a joke that doesn't work is obvious to everyone.

Due to stage inexperience, most presenters crumble when their joke doesn't work. They lean on the joke like a crutch and when it breaks, they collapse. Experienced comics go in the opposite direction; their job is just beginning when the joke doesn't fly. Johnny Carson is one of the best examples of making a joke work after it flopped. His response to the joke was more important, and more entertaining, than the joke itself.

For successful presentations, a sense of humor is much more important than comedy. Creating an open atmosphere of interaction, amusement, and unusual associations is more important than jokes. In order to create a sense of humor, begin in preproduction. Here are some ideas for creating a sense of humor:

- Have the audience members change chairs with the person next to them.
- Start the "wrong" speech (perhaps your acceptance of a party nomination or Academy Award).
- Remind specific audience members of their checkout times.
- Bring a pot of coffee with you onstage. Pour a cup as you begin your speech.
- As you begin, pay off a bet with an audience member—she didn't think you'd be ready for this speech.

- Explain to everyone that you are going to finish your presentation 15 minutes early—then make sure you do.

PRESENTATION PREPARATION

The art of effortlessness takes years to achieve. Improvisation builds several very useful attributes in presenters: responsiveness, intuition, empathy, understanding, and directed activity. Actors are taught, from the very beginning of their careers, to audition for everything. Get in on every audition whether or not the part is right for you. This advice has several benefits:

- Through constant auditioning, actors burn out the fear of rejection. They focus on the short-term task at hand—being great right now—as opposed to worrying about the effect on the auditors.
- Actors build an immediate energy that can be focused for the audition. Auditions are very short, five minutes maximum in most cases, so it's vital to tap into energy and concentration powers right now.
- Auditions are the key to an actor's future. It's easier to eat when you've got a job. So actors prepare extensively for that precious five minutes.

THERE IS NO SUBSTITUTE FOR REHEARSAL

Consider the preproduction elements that go into the creation of a Broadway theatrical production. Even after all the script revisions, staged readings, design, and other phases, the rehearsal process alone will be a minimum of eight weeks. This represents thousands of hours of rehearsal before any audience will see the show. Usually this is followed by previews of several weeks or months. These are professionally trained actors, the best in the world, who dedicate themselves to the flawless production of the show.

SIMPLE IMPROV-PRESENTING GAMES

These exercises and games sharpen improv-presenting skills for presenters:

- "One-Word Story." With a partner, create an original story with each partner contributing one word at a time. This game builds active listening and awareness and heightens the participants' speed of response.
- "Contrapuntal Debate." In a rehearsal setting, request an argument or thesis from your rehearsal group. The argument should be the opposite side of a commonly held position: The Sun revolves around the Earth; politeness is bad; Madonna is a great actress. Then commit to proving your point immediately and spontaneously. Commit to your character and position. You win the game if you convince the audience; you lose the game if you break character or the argument fails.
- "Expert Q&A." In a rehearsal setting, introduce yourself to your rehearsal group as an expert on a specific topic that you know well. It may be a hobby or interest you love. After a short thesis statement about the topic, have the audience grill you on your knowledge of the topic. Have them build in questions that *are not relevant* to the topic and deal with those answers as well.

CONCLUSION

Improvisation requires commitment, practice, confidence, and consistency, as do your presentations. Sharpen your skills through simple exercises and you will be able to apply them when needed. When all else fails, give the audience their money back.

CHAPTER 14

Managing Change

Here's a news flash from the "Really? No Kidding" Department: Virtually the only certainty in business is that what is reliable, permanent, and unwavering right now will change tomorrow.

The pervasive environment of change is perhaps the single most important aspect in business. This natural law of the business universe leads us to another inexorably accurate rule: As soon as we learn exactly how to do what we do, somebody changes the rules. It's not just Murphy's Law that prevails (whatever can go wrong will go wrong); it's also a maxim that even *things that go right* will change.

Webster's Dictionary offers this complex and detailed definition:

Change—to make different.

Everything moves, everything evolves, everything changes. This is good because if things didn't change they would stay the same, and if they stayed the same, nobody would ever get a promotion, hair plugs, or a pay raise. Instead of avoiding change, improvisers take the opposite tack. We implement mechanisms for change as an operating policy. We live change instead of it living us. From the category of Joe's Really Cool Aphorisms: It's not about changing our reactions; it's how we react to change that counts. Improvisation is a process to enact and/or manage change, a system by which you manage unknown information and stimuli. If we improvise properly, we will initiate, manage, and respond to change well. If we improvise poorly, we lose the power to adapt to and instigate our own changes.

A SAMPLE OF DEALING WITH CHANGE

In our lessons, you played the game called "One-Word Story," in which you and a partner begin to tell a story, each person contributing one word at a time. You don't know what they're going to say; they don't know what you're going to say. The story begins. It moves forward, around; it sputters and pauses, then picks back up again. As each player in the game lets go of logic, trusts the intuitive flow, and allows the story to exist, it picks up pace and meaning and direction. You build more agreement on a conscious and subconscious level. The story begins to delight you and your partner. Its very existence is improbable; its direction is impossible to predict. The story is funny and exciting and becoming more useful all the time. And you are improvising.

As a player/team, you are improv-operating in agreement on several levels of context:

- Speaking the same language (usually).
- Listening to each other to understand explicit and implicit directions of the story.
- Taking delight in each other's crazy/fun initiations and discoveries.
- Providing your partner with something fun, different, and exciting.
- Incorporating exploration as an operating methodology.

You are improvising—managing change while producing product. The energy of creation that is stimulated by this organic interaction builds even more attraction and interest in the creative process: Improvisers want to improvise more.

COMFORT/DISCOMFORT

None-too-shockingly, most people enjoy comfort: a good pair of shoes, a good car, an all-leather climate-controlled recliner, and a cold beer. Comfort is a nice feeling, a condition toward which we aim. And while comfort is great for your den, it's lousy for generating innovation and improvisation. In an improv-innovation environment, comfort breeds dullness, or worse, lameness: I'm comfortable; this works; it's easy; I've got it down cold. Comfort revels in familiarity, familiar is normal, and normal is what we've already got.

In order to innovatively improvise, we must suspend comfort and melt our perceptions of what was, forcing ourselves and our fellow players to move toward extraordinary areas, different results, unfamiliar expectation, and chaos. We learn to love chaos, reveling in a continuous flow of unexpected stimuli.

In order to allow ourselves to break away from our comfort zones, we improv toward antistructure, permitting ourselves to become uneasy, seeking the experience of new stimuli. As jazz is the edge of music, we improvise to the edge of activities, ideas, and innovation.

AN ASTONISHING STATE OF IMPROVISING

When you are immersed in improv activity, there's this superb sense of connection to yourself, to the work, and to your players. It's an activity of pure creation: act, absorb, initiate, act, move, absorb, and continue on and upward. This is the physical and strangely natural activity of improvisation in process.

- Act first.
- Accept input.
- Act on it.
- Initiate new activity.
- Act on that new stuff.
- Move away from what you've done.
- Absorb what it was.
- Act on something new.
- Absorb input from the work around you.
- Continue until you can't go on.

These steps are improvisation. As you act and initiate, you produce a phenomenon of "in this immediate time and space," the theatrical definition of "being in the moment." The occurrence is occurring as you are "occurring it." As you get better at generating the activities and initiations, as your speed of absorption increases, you achieve greater skills in each activity.

Every level of improv achievement carries its own rewards — you must build skills at the most basic levels of improvisation to move forward. It's like practicing scales on the piano: If you're good at the basics, you'll be better with the fancy stuff. And masters of the form make the scales sound like symphonies, anyway.

MASTER THE CONTEXT

Improv, at the beginning level, is loaded with concerns: fear of rejection, risk-aversion, struggles with form and function. New improvisers worry about the acceptance or rejection of the "end-product" of improvisation: Will the audience accept the results of the improv form? In comedy, this is manifested as trying to "please the audience." Get over this impulse right away. Kill it and move on.

Improvisation is about what you and your group are doing right now, not what someone else is perceiving that you're doing right now! Miles Davis had to please himself and his group first; the audience was a privileged participant, not the object of the exercise. Nothing of value can be created if you do not value it yourself. Do not ask someone to accept an initiation from you if you yourself don't care for it, love it, and think it's the best thing you've ever done.

SEPARATING JUDGMENT FROM THE CREATIVE PROCESS

We've agreed that improvisation, among many other things, is a system to increase the output of ideas. Because you're

189

incorporating stimuli from internal and external sources, improvisation taps into a wider range of options than "normal" or "regular" thinking. (Again, we want to burn down the box and think outside the remnants.) As we build the ability to incorporate more stimuli into our actions, we increase our output of thoughts, actions, ideas, and products.

As we accept this thesis—improv as an active idea generator—then we must ramp up our improvisation skills to build idea productivity to the highest output possible: Volume and repetition are everything. Simply put, the way to get better ideas is to first get more ideas. Greater output of ideas generates a higher quantity of quality ideas; more quality ideas allows for a larger pool for the selection/judgment process.

Is this just common sense? Maybe so, but this theory runs counter to many opinions of idea generation. Most people assume that good ideas are based on "inspiration," this accidental startling revelation, a brainwave, lightning bolt, or other random occurrence. While great ideas sometimes do appear from nowhere, ideas are *never* something you wait for: Directed activity and consistent repetition are the keys to idea generation. Improvisation is the activity. Through repetition of exercises and challenges, we build greater output of initiations. As we apply improv more and more, we build the ability to generate more something out of less nothing.

ARBITRATING AGREEMENT

The theories of improv rest firmly on the works of the brilliant, seminal teachers of improvisation for the theater: Viola Spolin, Bernie Sahlins, Keith Johnstone, David Shepherd, Paul Sills, Del Close, and many others, even Constantin Stanislavsky and

190

BRIEF DIGRESSION

Skeptics are now saying to themselves, "Yeah, yeah, I get it. We've all got to listen to each other and respect each other's opinion. I've got to play nice in the sandbox with the other kids."

Concurrence in our improvisation process must be continuous and arbitrary: Nobody can say "no" while we're improvising. This must be an internal rule as well as external. You can't *think* "no" while you're improvising and you can never think "no" of someone else's ideas. Your future success in improvisation depends on your ability to accept, develop, and heighten ideas from those around you. If you kill the idea in your brain, even before it really exists, you're destroying your own pipeline of new ideas.

As important, we have to train ourselves not only to make good ideas better but also to make bad ideas good. It's preposterously easy to "yes, and . . ." brilliant ideas, but appreciably harder to make something good out of a half-baked thought. In order to improvise brilliantly we must accept ideas no matter where they come from and for their *own* value, not the value we apply to them.

Great ideas are a force of will. Great idea-people, great improvisers are people who can *will something to be good*. No kidding: They choose to accept the idea, forward it, and mutate and elevate it. From this practice, great improvisers create the best things in our world. Great improvisers make the initiations and initiators around them better, faster, and more productive. Everyone is attracted to great improvisers: They're good listeners, they have interesting things to offer, they're usually funny, and they keep moving. We must model ourselves and our practices after them.

Jerzy Grotowski. While each of these pioneers had their own perspectives and applications of improv forms, all of them embraced and advocated a central tenet of improv: arbitrary agreement, the principle in which all participants must actively concur on the contextual premise of the activity, exercise, and challenge.

Through the consistent application of acceptance, players build an impetus of constant creative activity. These maxims must exist in the conscious state of activity: acceptance of rules, support of action, suspension of judgment, and other elements. But more important, arbitrary acceptance must be enacted by players on a subconscious basis. They must embed agreement as an operating methodology.

Arbitrary agreement should be embraced through a circle of applications:

- Agreement must be activated by players through acceptance, however chaotic and unexpected: "What is this thing?" "Show me that new plan." Players toss ideas and requests at each other unexpectedly and chaotically, and other players receive the initiations completely, comprehensively, and usefully.
- Players move, start, stop, and shift directions, requesting that fellow players jump and follow.

As improv processes and players struggle to find agreement, chaos enters the system. Random instigation of stimuli and activity leads players to radical themes and unusual directions. Loss of focus in the direction of the game is a frequent but tolerable result, as players struggle with the group mind and the chaos of stream of consciousness. We'll take chaos and manage it as opposed to holding on to normalcy.

Persevere through the stops, starts, and misdirections of improv and creative processes. They are a normal byproduct of innovative chaos. As players immerse themselves deeper in improv processes, they inevitably gravitate toward collective directions. As they work through, sweat through, suffer through, and enjoy their way through discoveries good and bad, they gravitate toward the center of the new circle, connecting, rewiring, linking to each other and to the group whole. As surely as combat teams and firefighter squads form bonds, improv artists shape themselves into a cohesive unit: *They become an ensemble.*

Conclusion

Technically, this isn't really a conclusion because improv doesn't end. Life changes, companies merge, mortgages get paid, you become your parents, but improv goes on into the great unknown. The universe transforms, initiates, agrees, accepts, explores, and adds to itself—we're the actors and somebody forgot to give us the script. So we improvise, adapt, and accept, moving forward into experience while building on our memories.

So:

- Go build great teams.
- Take risks.
- Support risk-takers.
- Nurture ideas.
- Separate judgment.
- Become curious.

- Build a useful, open environment.
- Invest time, space, and more time.
- Set goals.
- Let the ensemble be smarter than you.
- Build a sense of humor.
- Have and share fun.

If you do these things, you will become a great improviser and you'll have more fun doing it. I hope this book has been as much fun for you to read and use as it has been for me to write. Thanks for being part of my ensemble.

Yours improvisationally,
Joe Keefe

Suggested Readings

Days and Nights at the Second City, Bernie Sahlins (Chicago: Ivan R. Dee, 2001).

Improv, Keith Johnstone (New York: Routledge/Theatre Arts Books, 1979).

The Artist's Way, Julia Cameron (J. P. Tarcher, 1995).

Creators on Creating, edited by Frank Barron, Alfonso Montuori, Anthea Barron (New York: G. P. Putnam's Sons).

Being Irish . . . , Joe Keefe (Kansas City, MO: Andrews McMeel, 2002).

The 7 Habits of Highly Effective People, Stephen R. Covey (New York: Simon & Schuster, 1990).

SUGGESTED READINGS

Side Effects, Woody Allen (New York: Ballantine Books, 1989—reissue).

Improvisation for the Theater, Viola Spolin (Northwestern University Press, 1983—updated ed.).

198

Index

201